Plant-Based High-Protein Cookbook

Vegan Bodybuilding Diet Book for Athletic High-Protein Foods. 90 Recipes and 30-Day Meal Plan

Deborah Stephens

Table of Contents

Introduction. Plant Based Diet

Plant-based diets are becoming widely popular and more and more people are switching to plant based diets for a variety of reasons. Diets that are based on consumption of plant foods and are rich in beans, nuts, seeds, fruit and vegetables, whole grains, and cereal based foods can provide all the nutrients needed for good health and offer affordable, tasty and nutritious alternatives to meat based diets.

If you decided to switch to a plant based diet you might be worried about amount of protein you consume. People who already follow vegan diet have learned how to get all needed nutrients from plant foods and supplements. But you are probably wondering: where to get protein from if you do not eat meat, fish, eggs and dairy products? Animal protein contains all the essential amino acids our body needs. However, these acids can be also obtained from plant foods. What's more, a plant-based diet can significantly diversify your diet in terms of protein sources.

List of Plant Based High Protein Products

There is a common misconception that vegetarian and vegan diets might be lacking sufficient amount of protein. However, many dietitians and scientists say that vegetarian or vegan diets have more than enough nutrients in them if planned well. Nevertheless, all foods are different in their protein values, there is food that contains more protein, and there are those that contain less.

Legumes or commonly known as beans have high amounts of protein per serving and contain 15 grams of protein per cooked cup. They are also a great source of iron, complex carbohydrates, folate, fiber, phosphorus, manganese and potassium. Can be used in a variety of recipes or eaten without anything else.

Nutritional yeast is another great source of protein. It has 14 grams of protein per 28 grams. It is also a great source of copper, magnesium, zinc, manganese and all B vitamins. It can be used in a variety of dishes and is sold as flakes and a yellow powder.

Seitan, also known as wheat meat or wheat gluten is quite a popular source of protein. It is produced from gluten and contains about 25 grams of protein per 100 grams, which makes a very rich plant protein source. Seitan can be sautéed, fried, and even grilled and, thus, is really easy to incorporate in your favorite recipes.

Next come *lentils*. They have 18 grams of protein per cooked cup. They also can be added to a whole variety of dishes. Lentils are also rich in iron, manganese and folate.

Tempeh, tofu, and edamame are another great source of protein. They are made from whole soybeans, which means they provide all the important amino acids. All three have 10-19 grams of protein per 100 grams, calcium and iron. Edamame need to be steamed or boiled before eating and can be eaten without anything else or incorporated into soups and salads. Tofu and tempeh can also be used in lots of recipes.

Hempseed is another great source of protein. It contains 10 grams of protein per 28 grams. It is a good source of iron, magnesium, selenium, zinc, omega-3 and omega-6 fatty acids. It can be added to smoothies, salad dressings, morning muesli and protein bars.

Spelt and teff are from an ancient grains category. Teff is gluten-free, whereas spelt contains gluten. They have 10–11 grams of protein per cooked cup. Spelt and teff are rich in iron, zinc, magnesium, selenium, manganese, phosphorus, fiber, B vitamins, and complex carbs. They can be used in a whole variety of dishes.

Spirulina is a blue-green algae and is rich in protein. 2 tablespoons will provide 8 grams of protein. It will also cover 22% of the daily iron and thiamin need and 42% of the daily need of copper. It is also a good source of, riboflavin, magnesium, manganese, essential fatty acids and potassium.

Green peas have 9 grams of protein per cooked cup in them. Green peas is good choice to get magnesium, iron, zinc, phosphorus, B vitamins and copper. 1 serving of green peas has enough in it to cover 1/4 of the daily need for vitamin A, C, K, fiber, manganese, folate and thiamine. Can be used in a whole variety of recipes.

Quinoa and amaranth are ancient or gluten-free grains. They provide 8–9 grams of protein per cooked cup and are complete sources of protein. Amaranth and quinoa are also a good source of iron, complex carbs, fiber, phosphorus, magnesium and manganese. Can be used in a whole variety of recipes.

Ezekiel bread and other breads made from sprouted grains like wheat, millet, barley, spelt, soybeans and lentils are great choices of protein. 2 slices of Ezekiel bread contain 8 grams of protein. Sprouting can increase the bread's vitamin C, folate, soluble fiber, beta-carotene content and vitamin E. It may also slightly reduce the gluten content. Can be used in a whole variety of recipes.

Soy milk contains 7 grams of protein per cup and thus a good source of protein, but it's also an excellent source of calcium, vitamin D and vitamin B12, but only fortified milk contains vitamin B12, so make sure to buy that one. Can be consumed on its own or used in a variety of recipes.

Oats and oatmeal are standard in almost everyone's diet. ½ cup of dry oats provides 6 grams of protein and 4 grams of fiber. It is also a great source of zinc, folate, magnesium and phosphorus. Oats and oatmeal contain higher-quality protein than rice and wheat. Can be ground into flour, and used in a wide variety of recipes as flour and flakes.

Wild rice has more protein than other long-grain rice varieties, including brown rice and basmati. 1 cooked cup provides 7 grams of protein. It is also a good source of manganese, phosphorus fiber, copper, B vitamins and magnesium. Wild rice is not stripped of its bran and, thus, can contain arsenic in it. Therefore washing wild rice before cooking is a must, and boiling it in a large amount of water should reduce the possible level of arsenic.

Chia seeds provide 6 grams of protein and 13 grams of fiber per 35 grams. They are also a good source of iron, selenium, calcium, magnesium, antioxidants and omega-3 fatty acids.

Nuts, seeds and products from them provide between 5–7 grams of protein per 28 grams. They are also a great source of iron, healthy fats, calcium, fiber, phosphorus, magnesium, vitamin E selenium, certain B vitamins and antioxidants.

In this book you will find plant based high protein recipes for breakfast, lunch, dinner, snacks and desserts. In addition, you will have 4 weeks Meal Plan with shopping lists for each week

Breakfast

Skillet Potato and Tempeh Hash

Cooking Time: 40 minutes

Servings: 4

Ingredients

- 4 potatoes
- 1 onion, chopped
- 1 bell pepper, diced
- 8 oz. package tempeh, diced
- 5 leaves kale, stemmed and chopped
- 2 tablespoons olive oil
- 1 teaspoon all-purpose salt-free seasoning
- 1 teaspoon paprika
- 2 tablespoons nutritional yeast, optional
- salt and pepper, to taste

Instructions

1. Place potatoes in a parchment lined pan and bake until potatoes are firm. Remove from the oven and let cool, and finally dice potatoes.
2. Place a skillet over medium heat. Add oil.
3. To the skillet add onions and cook them for 2 minutes until translucent.
4. To the skillet add bell pepper, tempeh and diced potatoes. Sauté until turning golden brown.
5. Add kale and seasonings. Continue stirring, add water to keep potatoes from sticking to the pan.
6. To the skillet add nutritional yeast, salt and pepper to taste. Remove from heat.
7. Once done, serve.

Nutritional information (per serving): 268 calories; 8 g fat; 44 g total carbs; 9 g protein

High Protein Vegan French Toast

Cooking Time: 10 minutes

Servings: 1

Ingredients

- 6 oz. soy milk
- 1 scoop vanilla protein
- 2 tablespoons flax meal
- 2 teaspoons vanilla extract
- 1 teaspoon cinnamon
- 3 slices gluten-free bread

Instructions

1. In a large shallow bowl whisk soy milk, protein power, flax meal, vanilla extract and cinnamon.
2. Dip bread slices in the mixture until well coated.
3. Place a non-stick pan over medium heat. Cook toasts on the pan for 3 minutes on each side.
4. Serve topped with berries and syrup.

Nutritional information (per serving): 364 calories; 10 g fat; 33 g total carbs; 40 g protein

Pumpkin Chia Pancakes

Cooking Time: 20 minutes   **Servings:** 12

Ingredients

- 1 cup almond milk
- 1 tablespoon white vinegar
- 1 cup white whole wheat flour
- ½ cup pumpkin puree
- 2 teaspoons baking powder
- ½ teaspoon baking soda
- 1 teaspoon pumpkin pie spice
- 3 tablespoons chia seeds
- 1 flax egg
- 3 tablespoons coconut oil, melted and cooled slightly
- 1 tablespoon pure maple syrup
- 2 teaspoons pure vanilla extract
- ½ teaspoon kosher salt

Instructions

1. In a bowl whisk almond milk and vinegar. Set aside for 5 minutes.
2. In a small bowl combine 1 tablespoon flax meal with 3 tablespoons water. Set aside for 5 minutes to thicken. This substitutes the egg.
3. In a separate large bowl combine flour, baking powder, baking soda, pumpkin pie spice, chia seeds and salt. Combine well.
4. To the almond milk mix add flax egg, pumpkin, coconut oil, maple syrup and vanilla. Mix well.
5. Gradually add wet ingredients to dry ingredients.
6. Place a skillet over medium heat. Pour the batter and cook pancakes. Flip them when they begin to form bubbles for 2 minutes on each side.
7. Serve pancakes with desired toppings.

Nutritional information (per serving): 96 calories; 4.5 g fat; 12 g total carbs; 2 g protein

Blueberry Bliss Breakfast Bars

Raw

Cooking Time: 1 hour 10 minutes

Servings: 16

Ingredients

- 1 ½ cups gluten free rolled oats
- ¾ cup whole almonds
- ½ cup dried blueberries
- ½ cup pistachios
- ⅓ cup ground flaxseed
- ⅓ cup walnuts
- ⅓ cup pepitas
- ¼ cup sunflower seeds
- ⅓ cup pure maple syrup
- ¼ cup unsweetened apple sauce
- 1 cup almond butter

Instructions

1. Line a baking pan with parchment paper and make sure paper hangs over the edges.
2. In a large bowl combine rolled oats, almonds, blueberries, pistachios, flaxseed, pepitas, sunflower seeds and combine thoroughly.
3. To the bowl add maple syrup and continue mixing.
4. To the same bowl add almond butter and mix. Pour this batter in the prepared pan, press it down and freeze for 60 minutes
5. Remove from freezer, remove the parchment paper, cut into 8 bars, then slice the bar into half.
6. Once done, serve.

Nutritional information (per serving): 232 calories; 16 g fat; 15 g total carbs; 3.8 g protein

Chickpea Scramble Breakfast Bowl

Cooking Time: 25 minutes　　　　　　　**Servings:** 2

Ingredients

- 1 15 oz. can chickpeas
- ½ teaspoon turmeric
- ¼ onion, diced
- 2 cloves garlic, minced
- 1 teaspoon olive oil
- 1 packet mixed greens
- 1 handful of parsley minced
- 1 handful of cilantro minced
- 1 avocado. sliced
- salt and pepper

Instructions

1. To the medium bowl add chickpeas and some water. Mash with a fork, leaving some chickpeas whole.
2. Add turmeric, salt and pepper to the mashed chickpeas.
3. Place a pan over medium heat. Drizzle olive oil.
4. Add the onions and sauté them until soft.
5. Add garlic and cook for 1 minute making sure not to burn it
6. Add mashed chickpeas and cook for 5 minutes.
7. To serve add greens to the bottom of bowls, top with cooked chickpeas, cilantro, parsley and avocado slices.

Nutritional information (per serving): 500 calories; 23 g fat; 62 g total carbs; 18 g protein

Grain Salad with Blueberries Hazelnuts Lemon

Cooking Time: 8 hours 55 minutes

Servings: 8

Ingredients

- 1 cup steel-cut oats
- 1 cup dry golden quinoa
- ½ cup dry millet
- ½ cup maple syrup
- 1 cup vegan yogurt
- 2 cups hazelnuts, roughly chopped and toasted
- 2 cups blueberries or mixed berries
- 4 ½ cups water
- 3 tablespoons olive oil, divided
- 1-inch piece fresh ginger, peeled and sliced
- 2 teaspoons lemon zest
- 2 tablespoons lemon juice
- ¼ teaspoon nutmeg
- salt

Instructions

1. In a large bowl mix oats, quinoa and millet. Pour the mixture in a mesh strainer and place it under running water for about 60 seconds. Return to bowl and set aside.
2. Place a skillet over medium high heat. Add 1 tablespoon olive oil.
3. Add the mixed grains and cook for 3 minutes.
4. Add water, salt, ginger and 1 teaspoon lemon zest. Bring the mixture to a boil, cover, reduce heat and let it simmer for 20 minutes more. Remove from heat, fluff with fork and remove ginger.
5. Transfer cooked grains to a large baking dish and set aside for 30 minutes.
6. To a large bowl transfer cooled grains, add the remaining lemon zest.
7. In a separate bowl combine the remaining olive oil, lemon juice and stir well.
8. To the olive mixture stir in maple syrup, yoghurt and nutmeg. Pour this dressing over grains and mix well.
9. Add hazelnuts and blueberries and freeze in the refrigerator for 8-12 hours.
10. Once done, serve.

Nutritional information (per serving): 353 calories; 20 g fat; 38 g total carbs; 9.3 g protein

Peanut Butter Chia Overnight Oats

Cooking Time: 8 hours 5 minutes

Servings: 1

Ingredients

- ¾ cup rolled oats
- 1 cup unsweetened vanilla almond milk
- ½ cup filtered water
- 2 tablespoons chia seeds
- ½ teaspoon cinnamon
- 1 teaspoon vanilla extract
- 1 ripe banana, mashed
- 2 tablespoons PB Fit powder
- 1 ½ tablespoons water
- 2 tablespoons agave
- salt

Instructions

1. In a mason jar combine both oats, chia seeds, cinnamon and salt. Cover the jar and give it a good shake.
2. To the same jar add almond milk, water, vanilla, agave and mashed banana. Whisk well to combine.
3. In a bowl combine the PB powder and water until creamy and pour this mixturein to the mason jar.
4. Cover and refrigerate for 8-12 hours
5. Once done, serve.

Nutritional information (per serving): 533 calories; 16 g fat; 110 g total carbs; 16 g protein

Scrambled Tofu Breakfast

Burrito

Cooking Time: 30 minutes

Servings: 4

Ingredients

- *For Tofu:*
- 1 12-oz extra-firm tofu
- ¼ cup minced parsley
- 1 teaspoon oil
- 3 cloves garlic, minced
- 1 tablespoon hummus
- ½ teaspoon chili powder
- ½ teaspoon cumin
- 1 teaspoon nutritional yeast
- ¼ teaspoon sea salt
- *For Vegetables:*
- 2 cups chopped kale
- 5 whole baby potatoes, cubed
- 1 bell pepper, thinly sliced
- 1 teaspoon oil
- ½ teaspoon ground cumin
- ½ teaspoon chili powder
- 1 pinch sea salt
- For Burrito:
- 4 large flour gluten-free tortillas
- 1 ripe avocado, mashed
- cilantro
- chunky salsa

Instructions

1. Preheat the oven to 400 F and line a baking sheet with parchment paper.
2. Wrap tofu with a clean kitchen towel and place a heavy skillet on top of tofu to drain excess water. Crumble it.
3. Place potatoes and pepper on the baking sheet. Drizzle with oil and spices, toss to coat and place in the oven.
4. Bake for 22 minutes until soft. Add kale when it's about 6 minutes prior to the end.
5. Meanwhile place a skillet over medium heat. Add oil.
6. To the skillet add garlic, crumbled tofu and cook for 10 minutes until slightly browned.
7. In a medium bowl combine hummus, chili powder, cumin, nutritional yeast, salt and mix well.
8. Add 3 tablespoons water until a sauce is formed.
9. Add parsley and add this mixture to the tofu. Cook for 5 minutes and set aside.
10. To assemble on the tortilla add roasted vegetables, scrambled tofu, avocado, cilantro and salsa. Roll up burrito, place seam side down. Do this process with the remaining tortillas to make up 4 burritos.
11. Once done, serve.

Nutritional information (per serving): 441 calories; 16.5 g fat; 53.5 g total carbs; 16.5 g protein.

Hummus Toast

Cooking Time: 10 minutes

Servings: 1

Ingredients

- 2 slices sprouted wheat bread
- ¼ cup hummus
- 1 tablespoon hemp seeds
- 1 tablespoon unsalted sunflower seeds, roasted

Instructions

1. Toast bread in a toaster or in a skillet placed on high heat.
2. Place toasted bread on a serving plate, top with hummus, hemp seeds and sunflower seeds.
3. Once done, serve.

Nutritional information (per serving): 316 calories; 16 g fat; 24 g total carbs; 19 g protein

Chocolate Peanut Butter

Smoothie Bowl

Cooking Time: 5 minutes   **Servings:** 1

Ingredients

- *2 frozen bananas*
- *1/3 cup almond milk*
- *2 tablespoons peanut butter*
- *2 tablespoons cacao powder*
- *Optional add-ins:*
- *2 scoops vital proteins collagen*
- *2 teaspoons maca powder*
- *1 tablespoon chia seeds*
- *For topping:*
- *½ banana sliced*
- *chocolate granola*
- *peanut butter to drizzle*
- *chia seeds*

Instructions

1. To a blender add bananas, almond milk, peanut butter, cacao powder, collagen, maca powder and chia seeds. Pulse until smooth. Transfer to a bowl.
2. Add your favorite toppings.
3. Once done, serve.

Nutritional information (per serving): 485 calories; 19 g fat; 79 g total carbs; 13 g protein

Greek Chickpeas On Toast

Cooking Time: 30 minutes

Servings: 2

Ingredients

- 2 cups chickpeas, cooked
- 6 slices gluten free crusty bread, toasted
- 2 tablespoons olive oil
- 3 shallots, diced
- 2 garlic cloves, diced
- ¼ teaspoon smoked paprika
- ½ teaspoon sweet paprika
- ½ teaspoon cinnamon
- 1 teaspoon sugar
- 2 large tomatoes, skinned and chopped
- fresh parsley, to garnish
- 1 tablespoon pitted Kalamata olives, to garnish
- salt and pepper

Instructions

1. Place a skillet over medium heat. Add olive oil.
2. To the skillet add shallots and cook until almost translucent.
3. Add garlic and continue cooking until shallots are translucent and soft.
4. Add spices and cook for 2 minutes while stirring frequently.
5. Add tomatoes to the skillet with some water. Reduce heat to low and let the sauce simmer until nicely thickened.
6. Add cooked chickpeas, sugar, salt and pepper. Cook for about 2 minutes. Remove from heat.
7. Serve on toasted bread with a drizzle of parsley and some olives.

Nutritional information (per serving): 623 calories; 21 g fat; 90 g total carbs; 23 g protein

Quinoa With Chai Spiced

Almond Milk Cinnamon

Cooking Time: 25 minutes   **Servings:** 1

Ingredients

- ½ cup quinoa, well rinsed
- 1 cup unsweetened almond milk
- 1 chai tea bag
- ½ tablespoon coconut palm sugar
- optional toppings, pecans, coconut flakes and ½ teaspoon cinnamon

Instructions

1. Place a medium skillet over medium heat.
2. Add almond milk, quinoa and chai tea bag. Bring mixture to a boil.
3. Remove tea bag and stir in coconut palm sugar, which is optional. Reduce heat and let it simmer for about 20 minutes while covered.
4. Serve in breakfast bowl topped with pecans, coconut and cinnamon.

Nutritional information (per serving): 406 calories; 8 g fat; 71 g total carbs; 13 g protein

Spicy Scrambled Tofu Breakfast Tacos

Cooking Time: 20 minutes   **Servings:** 3

Ingredients

- 1 16-oz. block extra-firm tofu, drained and rinsed
- ½ cup jarred roasted bell pepper, chopped
- ½ tablespoon olive oil
- 1 poblano pepper, cored and diced
- ½ onion, diced
- 3 Roma tomatoes
- 1 tablespoon chili powder
- 1 tablespoon smoked paprika
- 2 tablespoons lime juice
- 10 small corn tortillas, warmed
- 1 ripe avocado, halved, pitted, peeled, and mashed with sea salt + lime juice to taste
- cilantro leaves
- salt

Instructions

1. Place a large skillet over medium heat. Add olive oil.
2. To the skillet add poblano pepper and onions. Sauté for 6 minutes until soften.
3. To a blender add Roma tomatoes and blend until a puree is formed. Set aside.
4. To the skillet add pepper, chili powder, smoked paprika and salt. Continue cooking for 60 seconds.
5. To the skillet add pureed tomatoes, and crumble in tofu. Let it simmer for about 10 minutes until liquid reduces, do not forget to stir occasionally.
6. Add in lime juice and cook for 2 minutes. Remove from heat.
7. Scoop the tofu filling and place into warm tortilla, top with mashed avocado and a sprinkle of cilantro. Once done, serve.

Nutritional information (per serving): 490 calories; 24 g fat; 55 g total carbs; 24 g protein

Peanut Butter Jelly Overnight Oats

Cooking Time: 8 hours 10 minutes   **Servings:** 1

Ingredients

- *For Berry Chia Jam:*
- *2 cups frozen berries*
- *¼ cup water*
- *4 tablespoons chia seeds*
- *4 tablespoons maple syrup*
- *2 teaspoon vanilla extract*
- *Peanut butter and jelly oats:*
- *1 cup old-fashioned rolled oats*
- *1 1/2 cups almond milk*
- *2 tablespoons peanut butter*
- *1 scoop vanilla protein powder*
- *pinch of sea salt*
- *1 batch of berry chia jam*

Instructions

1. To prepare the berry chia jam place a skillet over medium low heat.
2. Add berries and water to the skillet, stir and break berries to form puree.
3. While berries are tender add the rest of the ingredients. Remove from heat and set aside to cool for about 10 minutes while stirring frequently, then transfer jam to mason jar. (Prepare the day before).
4. In a medium bowl combine oats, almond milk, protein powder and salt. Stir well and place in the refrigerator for 8-12 hours.
5. Serve one layer of ¼ of overnight oats, top with ¼ layer of berry chia jam, another layer of ¼ of overnight oats and more berry chia jam.
6. Drizzle peanut butter jam on top. Enjoy!

Nutritional information (per serving): 402 calories; 14 g fat; 55 g total carbs; 19 g protein

Fluffy Protein Pancakes

Cooking Time: 10 minutes

Servings: 2

Ingredients

- 1 cup all-purpose flour
- ¼ cup vegan protein powder
- 1 cup water, plus more as needed
- 1 tablespoon baking powder
- 2 tablespoons maple syrup, see notes
- ½ teaspoon sea salt

Instructions

1. In a large bowl combine flour, protein powder, baking powder and salt. Mix well.
2. To the bowl add maple syrup and stir. Gradually add water, stir until the mixture is thick and lumpy, set aside for 5 minutes.
3. Place pan over medium heat. Grease with cooking spray and pour batter.
4. Cook pancakes until bubbles start to appear at the edges, flip and cook the other side for 2 minutes.
5. Serve with your favorite topping, berries, sliced bananas and maple syrup.

Nutritional information (per serving): 295 calories; 1.2 g fat; 60 g total carbs; 16 g protein

Simple Vegan Omelet

Cooking Time: 30 minutes   **Servings:** 2

Ingredients

- *For Omelet:*
- 5 oz. firm silken tofu, drained and gently patted dry
- 2 tablespoons hummus
- 2 large cloves garlic, minced
- 2 tablespoons nutritional yeast
- ¼ teaspoon paprika
- 1 teaspoon cornstarch powder
- salt and pepper
- *For Filling:*
- *1* heaping cup veggies of choice (onion, tomato, mushroom, spinach)
- For Toppings (optional):
- 1 handful cilantro
- 2 tablespoons salsa
- 2 tablespoons vegan parmesan cheese

Instructions

1. Preheat the oven to 375 degrees F.
2. Prepare vegetables by slicing onions, tomatoes, mushroom and spinach, set aside.
3. Place an oven safe skillet over medium heat. Add olive oil and garlic, cook until it browns, then transfer to a food processor.
4. To the food processor add the rest of the omelet ingredients, add 2 tablespoons of water and pulse. Set aside.
5. Return skillet to medium heat. Add oil and onions.
6. To the skillet add tomatoes, mushrooms, spinach, salt and pepper. Cook until tender and set aside.
7. Add back ¼ of the cooked vegetables to the skillet and spoon the omelet batter, spread the batter carefully and cook for 5 minutes, remove from heat and place skillet in the oven for 15 minutes until the omelet is well done. Remove from oven.
8. Serve topped with toast, salsa, cheese and cilantro.

Nutritional information (per serving): 232 calories; 8 g fat; 22 g total carbs; 2 g protein

Veggie Sausage Patties

Cooking Time: 30 minutes   **Servings:** 5

Ingredients

- 1 can (15 oz.) chickpeas
- 2-3 cloves garlic peeled and chopped
- 1 teaspoon turmeric
- 1 teaspoon fennel seeds
- 1 teaspoon caraway seeds
- 1 teaspoon dried sage
- 1 tablespoon ground flax seeds
- 2 tablespoons water
- 1 tablespoon tamari sauce
- salt and pepper to taste

Instructions

1. Preheat the oven to 300 degrees F.
2. To a food processor add all the above ingredients and pulse until thick mixture is formed and set aside.
3. Place a skillet over medium heat, grease it with non-stick cooking spray.
4. Scoop one spoon of the chickpea mixture and place it on the skillet, shape it like a burger patty, season with paprika, salt and pepper, cook for 5 minutes on each side.
5. Place cooked patties on a parchment lined baking sheet. Place in the oven for 15 minutes. Remove from oven and let it cool. Serve warm.

Nutritional information (per serving): 90 calories; 18 g fat; 13 g total carbs; 5 g protein

Jumbo Chickpea Pancake

Cooking Time: 10 minutes   **Servings:** 1

Ingredients

- ¼ cup onion, finely chopped
- ¼ cup finely chopped red pepper
- ½ cup chickpea flour
- ½ cup + 2 tablespoons water
- ¼ teaspoon garlic powder
- ¼ teaspoon baking powder
- 1 pinch red pepper flakes (optional)
- salt and pepper

Instructions

1. Place a skillet over medium heat.
2. In a small bowl combine chickpea flour, garlic powder, baking powder, red pepper flakes, salt and pepper. Mix well.
3. To the small bowl add water and whisk it until air bubbles form in the batter.
4. Add chopped vegetables to the batter.
5. Grease the hot skillet with non-stick cooking spray.
6. Pour batter in the skillet and spread it out, cook for 5 minutes on each side until golden.
7. Serve pancakes with your desired toppings.

Nutritional information (per serving): 100 calories; 1.5 g fat; 15 g total carbs; 5 g protein

Simple Tofu Quiche

Cooking Time: 1 hour 45 minutes   **Servings:** 8

Ingredients

For Crust:
- 3 cups potatoes, grated
- 2 tablespoons vegan butter, melted
- salt and pepper

For Filling:
- 12.3 oz. extra-firm silken tofu, patted dry
- ¾ cup tomatoes, halved
- 1 cup broccoli, chopped
- 3 cloves garlic, chopped
- 2 leeks, sliced
- 2 tablespoons nutritional yeast
- 3 tablespoons hummus
- salt and pepper

Instructions

1. Preheat the oven to 450 F, and grease a pie pan with non-stick cooking spray.
2. Place grated potatoes on a clean kitchen towel, firmly squeeze the excess moisture and place in the greased dish.
3. Drizzle vegan butter, salt and pepper. Toss to coat.
4. Place in the oven and bake for ½ hour, remove crust from the oven and reduce temperature to 400 F.
5. To the baking sheet add vegetables, garlic, drizzle 2 tablespoons olive oil, salt and pepper. Place in the oven and bake for ½ hour. Remove from the oven and lower heat to 375 F.
6. To make the filling, add nutritional yeast, hummus, salt and pepper to a food processor, pulse and set aside.
7. In a large mixing bowl combine vegetables and the tofu mixture. Add this layer to the crust, spread to an even layer. Return to the oven and bake quiche at 375 F for 40 minutes until the top part is well browned.
8. Remove from the oven and set aside to cool. Serve!

Nutritional information (per serving): 178 calories; 9 g fat; 20 g total carbs; 7 g protein

Spiced Pumpkin Oatmeal

Cooking Time: 7 minutes

Servings: 1

Ingredients

For oatmeal:
- 1 cup almond milk
- ½ cup water
- ½ cup regular rolled oats
- ¼ cup pumpkin puree
- ¼ teaspoons vanilla extract
- ½ teaspoons pumpkin pie spice
- 2 teaspoons maple syrup
- 1 pinch of salt

For Java PB2:
- 3 tablespoons PB2
- water
- ¼ teaspoon instant coffee granules

Instructions

1. To a deep sauce pan add almond milk, water and bring to a boil over medium heat.
2. Add oats and reduce heat to low. Cook for 2 minutes and add pumpkin puree. Stir.
3. Meanwhile in a small bowl combine water, 3 tablespoons PB2 and instant coffee granules. Stir until thick and spreadable.
4. To the oatmeal, while the liquid is dissolving add vanilla extract, pumpkin pie spice, maple syrup and salt. Mix well.
5. Serve the oatmeal, top with java PB2 and any of toppings.

Nutritional information (per serving): 293 calories; 5 g fat; 55 g total carbs; 7 g protein

Pear Banana Loaf

Cooking Time: 50 minutes

Servings: 4

Ingredients

- ¾ cup chickpea flour
- ¾ cup oat flour
- ¾ cup almond meal
- 2 teaspoons baking powder
- ¾ teaspoon baking soda
- ½ teaspoon ground cinnamon
- 1 ½ cups ripe pears, peeled, chopped and divided
- ¾ cup ripe banana, sliced
- 6 tablespoons pure maple syrup
- 1 tablespoon fresh lemon juice
- 1 ½ teaspoons pure vanilla extract
- ¼ teaspoon sea salt

Instructions

1. Preheat the oven to 350 F and line a loaf pan with parchment paper, let the paper hang over the edges.
2. In a bowl combine chickpea flour, oat flour, almond meal, baking powder, baking soda, cinnamon and salt. Set the mixture aside.
3. To a food processor add ¾ cup pear, banana, maple syrup, lemon juice and vanilla until smooth. Transfer this to the dry ingredients, combine well.
4. Fold in ¾ cup pear and transfer the batter to the prepared pan, level the layer.
5. Place in the oven and bake for 45 minutes, set aside to cool. Slice and serve.

Nutritional information (per serving): 427 calories; 4 g fat; 89 g total carbs; 10 g protein

33

Vegan Blueberry Flax Muffins

Cooking Time: 50 minutes   **Servings:** 12

Ingredients

- 2 cups oat flour
- ¼ cup ground flax
- 1 cup almond milk
- ½ cup applesauce
- ½ cup brown sugar
- 1/3 cup maple syrup
- 1 ½ cups blueberries
- 2 teaspoons baking powder
- 1 teaspoon vanilla extract
- 4 tablespoons coconut oil, melted
- 1 teaspoon vinegar
- salt

Instructions

1. Preheat the oven to 375 F and grease a 12-muffin pan with non-stick cooking spray.
2. In a small bowl combine almond milk and vinegar. Set aside for 10 minutes to curdle.
3. In a large bowl mix flour, flax seed, baking powder, salt and cinnamon.
4. To the flour mix add applesauce, melted coconut oil, maple syrup, almond mixture. Mix well, then fold in blueberries.
5. Transfer batter to the 12-tin muffin tray, fill up to ¾.
6. Bake for 30-35 minutes until golden brown.
7. Serve while warm.

Nutritional information (per serving): 193 calories; 6 g fat; 32 g total carbs; 3 g protein

Rosemary Fig Scones

Cooking Time: 20 minutes

Servings: 8

Ingredients

- 1/2 cup coconut oil, cold
- 2 cups brown rice flour
- 1 cup milk, non-dairy
- 1/4 cup coconut sugar
- 3 tablespoons rosemary, chopped
- 1 tablespoon baking powder
- 1/2 cup dried figs, chopped
- 1 tablespoon lemon zest
- 1/4 teaspoon salt

Instructions

1. Preheat the oven to 350 F.
2. Combine milk together with rosemary and lemon zest in a bowl, set aside.
3. Combine brown rice flour together with coconut sugar, salt, baking powder and cold coconut in a bowl.
4. Using pastry cutter or a fork, mix coconut oil into flour mixture making sure that the mixture is even throughout with small coconut oil, then add in dried figs.
5. Combine the wet and dry ingredients with your hands, knead dough, ensuring that the dough is slightly sticky. Add more flour or milk to the dough if it's too sticky or too dry.
6. Roll out the dough on a well-floured surface into a circle that is about 1 ½ inches thick, then cut the dough into eight equally-sized pieces using a pizza cutter.
7. Place them onto a baking sheet lined with a parchment paper, bake for about 18 minutes. Serve and enjoy!

Nutritional Info (Per Serving): 173 calories; 14.8 g fat; 11 g total carbs; 1 g protein

Carrot Cake Waffles

Cooking Time: 50 minutes

Servings: 4

Ingredients

- 3/4 cup almond milk
- 1 cup flour, gluten-free
- 2 ½ tablespoons warm water
- 1 teaspoon baking powder
- 1/2 cup carrots, finely grated
- 1 pinch salt
- 1/4 cup pineapple, crushed
- 1 pinch ground ginger
- 1/2 teaspoon cinnamon
- 1 teaspoon white or apple cider vinegar
- 2 tablespoon coconut sugar
- 1 ½ tablespoon ground flax seeds
- 2 tablespoon coconut flakes

Instructions

1. Preheat a waffle iron to medium-high.
2. Add vinegar to almond milk to make buttermilk, then add warm water to flax to make an egg.
3. Combine all the dry ingredients in a bowl and stir them together until combined.
4. Add the prepared buttermilk, crushed pineapple and coconut to the dry ingredients and stir. Stir in the flax egg and grated carrot.
5. Add batter to the waffle maker and cook for about 5 minutes. Serve with toppings of choice and enjoy!

Nutritional Info (Per Serving): 218 calories; 5.3 g fat; 37 g total carbs; 6 g protein

Protein Dessert Pizza

Cooking Time: 25 minutes

Servings: 4

Ingredients

- For the crust:
- ¼ cup cacao powder
- 1 scoop vegan protein powder chocolate flavor
- ¼ cup chickpea flour
- 2 tablespoons maple syrup
- 2 tablespoons coconut oil
- For the cream:
- ½ teaspoon vanilla extract
- 1 cup coconut cream
- 1 tablespoon maple syrup
- For the jam:
- 1 tablespoon lemon juice
- 12 oz. raspberries, fresh
- 1 lemon, zested

Instructions

1. Preheat the oven to 350F.
2. Combine protein powder together with chickpea flour and cacao powder in a bowl, then mix the melted coconut oil together with maple syrup in a small bowl. Pour the melted coconut oil mixture over the dry mixture and mix well until smooth.
3. Form the mixture into a ball, then roll out the formed ball into a thin circle and place on a baking sheet lined with parchment paper. Bake for about 12-14 minutes, then let cool.
4. Combine the raspberries together with lemon zest and lemon juice in a pot, then bring to a boil. Allow to simmer as you stir to break up the berries until a jam-like consistency is formed. Allow to cool.
5. Beat coconut milk in a bowl on high until stiff peaks form, about 1-2 minutes. Add in maple syrup and vanilla extract and beat well until combined.
6. When the crust has cooled, cut it into 8 even pieces and top each slice with the coconut cream, fresh raspberries and raspberry jam. Serve and enjoy!

Nutritional Info (Per Serving): 412 calories; 28.8 g fat; 42 g total carbs; 5 g protein

Protein Carrot Cake

Cooking Time: 10 minutes

Servings: 4

Ingredients

For the cake:
- ½ cup ground almonds
- 2 carrots
- ¼ teaspoon ground nutmeg
- ½ cup dried coconut
- 1 teaspoon cinnamon
- 1-2 teaspoons stevia
- 2 tablespoons orange juice
- 2 tablespoons orange zest
- 3 tablespoons vanilla protein powder
- ½ cup pecans
- ½ cup raisins

For the frosting:
- 2 tablespoons coconut oil
- 2 cups cashews, soaked
- 2 tablespoons maple syrup
- 2 tablespoons lemon juice
- Water, if necessary

Instructions

1. Prepare the cake. Add all the ingredients for the cake to a food processor and pulse until well blended. Press the blended mix into a cake pan.
2. Prepare the frosting. Add all the ingredients for the frosting to a food processor and pulse until blended as you add water to achieve the desired consistency. Refrigerate before serving.
3. Top the cake with frosting and serve. Enjoy!

Nutritional Info (Per Serving): 235 calories; 17.4 g fat; 17 g total carbs; 6 g protein

Rice Crispies Pucks

Cooking Time: 10 minutes

Servings: 4

Ingredients

- 3 tablespoons creamy nut or seed butter
- 2 cups crisp rice cereal
- 3 tablespoons brown rice syrup
- 1/4 cup vanilla protein powder, plant-based
- 1-2 tablespoons semisweet chocolate chips, melted

Instructions

1. Spray or grease 8 cups muffin tin.
2. Stir the cereal together with protein powder in a bowl.
3. Cook the nut or seed butter and syrup in a saucepan over medium heat as you stir until the mixture begins to bubble. Cook as you stir for additional 30 seconds. Pour over the cereal mixture.
4. Scoop into the 8 cups of standard muffin tin.
5. Allow to cool completely, then remove from the muffin cups. Drizzle with the melted chocolate and serve. Enjoy!

Nutritional Info (Per Serving): 199 calories; 10.1 g fat; 20 g total carbs; 8 g protein

Lunch

High Protein Salad

Cooking Time: 5 minutes

Servings: 8

Ingredients

For the salad:
- 4 tablespoons capers
- 15 oz. canned green or red kidney beans
- 2 handfuls arugula
- 15 oz. canned lentils

For the dressing:
- 1 tablespoon tahini
- 1 tablespoon caper brine
- 1 tablespoon balsamic vinegar
- 2 tablespoons peanut butter
- 2 tablespoons hot sauce
- 1 tablespoon tamari
-

Instructions

1. Prepare the dressing. Whisk all the ingredients for the dressing in a bowl until smooth.
2. Prepare the salad. Mix the beans together with lentils arugula and capers.
3. Top the salad with the dressing and serve. Enjoy!

Nutritional Info (Per Serving): 128 calories; 2.3 g fat; 22 g total carbs; 9 g protein

Tempeh Tacos

Cooking Time: 20 minutes   **Servings:** 6

Ingredients

- 8 oz tempeh, chopped, fried
- 6 taco shells
    For Asian Slaw:
- 1 cup carrots, grated
- 1 cup green cabbage, shredded
- 3 scallions, chopped
- 1 cup red cabbage, shredded
    For Dressing:
- 1 tablespoon Dijon mustard
- 1/4 cup apple cider vinegar
- 1 tablespoon maple syrup
- 2 tablespoons sesame oil or extra virgin olive oil
- 1/4 teaspoon salt
- 1 tablespoon lime juice
- 1 tablespoon sriracha
- 1/4 teaspoon pepper
- 1/2 tablespoon tamari
-

Instructions

1. Add all the ingredients for the dressing into a bowl, then whisk well until combined.
2. Combine the slaw ingredients together in a bowl and mix until coated.
3. Take the taco shells and add slaw, then top with the tempeh. Drizzle with hot sauce or teriyaki sauce to taste. Serve and enjoy!

Nutritional Info (Per Serving): 216 calories; 13 g fat; 15 g total carbs; 10 g protein

Chickpeas Edamame Salad

Cooking Time: 5 minutes | **Servings:** 4

Ingredients

- 1/3 cup green pepper, chopped
- 2 (15.5 oz.) cans chickpeas, rinsed and drained
- 1/4 cup carrots, diced
- 3/4 cup edamame soy beans
- 1/3 cup red pepper, chopped
- 1 garlic clove, minced
- 3 tablespoons dried cranberries
  For Dressing:
- 1 teaspoon sugar
- 2 tablespoons grapeseed oil
- 1/4 teaspoon dried rosemary
- 1/4 teaspoon dried oregano
- 2 tablespoons olive oil
- Salt and pepper, to taste
- 1 teaspoon white vinegar
- 1/4 teaspoon dried basil

Instructions

1. Combine chickpeas together with edamame, green pepper, red pepper, carrots, minced garlic and dried cranberries in a bowl. Set aside.
2. Combine grapeseed oil together with olive oil, oregano, vinegar, sugar, rosemary and basil in another bowl and whisk until blended.
3. Pour the prepared dressing over the chickpeas and toss gently.
4. Season with salt and pepper to taste, chill for 30 minutes. Serve chilled and enjoy!

Nutritional Info (Per Serving): 345 calories; 17.3 g fat; 36 g total carbs; 14 g protein

Avocado White Bean Salad

Cooking Time: 5 minutes   **Servings:** 4

Ingredients

For the salad:
- 1 Roma tomato, chopped
- 1 avocado, chopped
- ¼ sweet onion, chopped
- 1 can white beans
For the vinaigrette:
- 1 teaspoon mustard
- 1 ½ tablespoons olive oil
- Salt and pepper, to taste
- 1/4 cup lemon juice
- Garlic, chopped to taste
- Basil, fresh or dried to taste
-

Instructions

1. Whisk together all the ingredients for the vinaigrette, then pour over the salad base. Mix well.
2. Refrigerate for few hours then serve. Enjoy!

Nutritional Info (Per Serving): 147 calories; 12.6 g fat; 9 g total carbs; 2 g protein

Arugula Lentil Salad

Cooking Time: 7 minutes   **Servings:** 2

Ingredients

- 1 cup brown lentils, cooked
- ¾ cups cashews
- 3 slices bread, whole wheat
- 1 onion
- 3 tablespoons olive oil
- 1 handful arugula
- 5-6 sun-dried tomatoes in oil
- 1 jalapeño
- 1-2 tablespoons balsamic vinegar
- Salt and pepper, to taste

Instructions

1. Roast cashews in a pan over low heat for about 3 minutes, then transfer them into a salad bowl.
2. Dice the onion and fry in oil on low heat for about 3 minutes.
3. In the meantime, chop jalapeno and dried tomatoes, then add them to the pan with cooking onions. Allow to cook for additional 1-2 minutes.
4. Cut bread into croutons and move the onion mix into a big bowl.
5. Add all the remaining oil to the pan and add in chopped bread. Cook until crunchy, then season with salt and pepper to taste.
6. Wash arugula and add it to the bowl with the onion mix, then add in lentils. Mix them well and season with salt, balsamic vinegar and pepper.
7. Serve with the croutons and enjoy!

Nutritional Info (Per Serving): 663 calories; 41 g fat; 64 g total carbs; 25 g protein

Maple Tempeh with Carrot Slaw

Cooking Time: 5 minutes

Servings: 8

Ingredients

- 4 cups carrots, shredded
- 8 oz. tempeh, sliced into triangles
- 2-3 teaspoons tamari
- ¼ teaspoon liquid smoke
- 1/4 teaspoon turmeric powder
- 1 ½ tablespoon maple syrup
- 1/8 teaspoon black pepper
- 1 tablespoon raw walnuts, crushed
- 1/4 cup lemon juice
- 1 onion, diced
- 1 teaspoon olive oil
- 1 tablespoon curry powder
- 1 ½ tablespoons maple syrup
- 2 tablespoons tahini
- Salt and pepper, to taste
- 1/2 cup flat leaf parsley, chopped

Instructions

1. Preheat oil in a skillet over high heat.
2. Add tempeh triangles to the hot oil along with tamari, maple and the liquid smoke. Flip tempeh, cook for about 5 minutes as you flip the tempeh a few times during the cooking process.
3. Turn the heat off when the tempeh has browned, then sprinkle with black pepper and add walnut pieces over the tempeh. Set the pan aside.
4. Add carrots to a large mixing bowl along with tahini, spices, lemon juice, maple syrup, onion, and parsley, then toss well for a few minutes to marinate carrots in the dressing.
5. Add salt and pepper to the carrot salad to taste. Serve carrot salad in a bowl and top with tempeh.

Nutritional Info (Per Serving): 263 calories; 12.8 g fat; 27 g total carbs; 14 g protein

Tofu Chili

Cooking Time: 30 minutes

Servings: 4

Ingredients

- 3 garlic cloves, minced
- 3 tablespoons vegetable oil
- 3 tablespoons chili powder
- 1 (14 oz.) package tofu, crumbled
- 1 (14 oz.) can tomato sauce
- 1 onion, diced
- 1/2 teaspoon cumin
- 1 green bell pepper, diced
- 1 cup mushrooms, sliced
- 1 (28 oz.) can kidney beans, drained
- 1/4 teaspoon cayenne pepper
- 1 (28 oz.) can tomatoes, undrained
- Salt and pepper, to taste
- 1 tablespoon sugar, optional

Instructions

1. Preheat 3 tablespoons vegetable oil in a pan, sauté the tofu in a pot over medium-high heat for about 3 minutes.
2. Add onion to the pot with tofu along with green pepper, garlic, 3 tablespoons of chili powder, 1 cup mushrooms, ¼ teaspoon of cayenne, ½ teaspoon of cumin, salt and pepper. Allow to cook for about 5 minutes until the veggies are slightly tender.
3. Add tomato sauce to the pot along with the diced or whole tomatoes, optional 1 tablespoon of sugar and the kidney beans. Bring to a slow simmer, then closed the lid. Allow to cook for 15 minutes or more until doneness. Serve and enjoy!

Nutritional Info (Per Serving): 289 calories; 18.8 g fat; 28 g total carbs; 8 g protein

Lentil Soup

Cooking Time: 50 minutes   **Servings:** 4

Ingredients

- 1 carrot, sliced
- 1 teaspoon vegetable oil
- 1 cup brown lentils, uncooked
- 1 onion, diced
- 2 bay leaves
- 1 dash pepper, to taste
- 4 cups vegetable broth
- Salt, to taste
- 2 teaspoon lemon juice
- 1/4 teaspoon dried thyme

Instructions

1. Sauté carrots and onions in oil in a large pot, for about 3-5 minutes.
2. Add vegetable broth to the cooking pot along with lentils, bay leaves, thyme, a dash of salt and pepper. Reduce the heat to simmer and close the lid. Allow to cook for about 45 minutes until the lentils are soft.
3. Remove the bay leaves. Stir in lemon juice if using to bring all the other flavors a bit more.
4. Taste and adjust salt and pepper. Enjoy!

Nutritional Info (Per Serving): 147 calories; 11.3 g fat; 8 g total carbs; 12 g protein

Black Bean and Sweet Potato Chili

Cooking Time: 25 minutes

Servings: 6

Ingredients

- 2 tablespoons olive oil
- 2 carrots, sliced
- 2 garlic cloves, minced
- 1 tablespoon chili powder
- 1 teaspoon cumin
- 1 onion, diced
- 1/2 cup water or vegetable broth
- 2 sweet potatoes, peeled, chopped
- 1/2 teaspoon cayenne, or to taste
- 1/2 red bell pepper, chopped
- 1/2 teaspoon garlic powder
- 1 (15 oz.) can black beans
- 1/2 teaspoon salt
- 1 (15 oz.) can diced tomatoes or tomato sauce
- 1/4 teaspoon black pepper

Instructions

1. Saute onions and garlic in olive oil in a soup pot or a Dutch oven for about 1-2 minutes.
2. Add chopped sweet potatoes to the cooking pan along with sliced carrots and chopped bell pepper. Allow to cook for about 5-6 minutes until the onions are soft.
3. Reduce the heat to medium-low heat. Add all the remaining ingredients to the cooking pan as you stir until well combined.
4. Let the chili simmer over medium-low heat partially covered and as you stir occasionally, for about 20-25 minutes.
5. Serve the chilli and top with your desired toppings. Enjoy!

Nutritional Info (Per Serving): 186 calories; 5.3 g fat; 10 g total carbs; 12 g protein

Black Bean Soup

Cooking Time: 10 minutes

Servings: 4

Ingredients

- 1/2 cup salsa
- 2 (15 oz.) cans black beans, undrained
- 1 tablespoon chili powder
- 16 oz. vegetable broth

Instructions

1. Mash one can of the black beans or pulse the beans with little extra water in a food processor until they are mostly smooth.
2. Pour both cans of beans into a saucepan, and add in vegetable broth, chili powder and salsa.
3. Bring everything to a boil. Once boiled, serve the soup topped with cilantro and onion if desired. Enjoy!

Nutritional Info (Per Serving): 124 calories; 14.4 g fat; 9 g total carbs; 2 g protein

Vegetable Quinoa Minestrone

Cooking Time: 30 minutes   **Servings:** 4-6

Ingredients

- 1/4 cup white quinoa, uncooked
- 1 tablespoon olive oil
- 1 cup carrots, sliced
- 3 garlic cloves, minced
- 2 bay leaves
- 1 small white onion, diced
- 1 cup zucchini, chopped
- 1 (28 oz.) can tomatoes, diced
- 1 1/2 cups asparagus, chopped
- 4 cups water or vegetable broth
- 2 teaspoons Italian seasoning
- 1/2 cup peas, frozen
- 1 cup packed kale or spinach, chopped
- Salt and pepper, to taste
- Nutritional yeast or parmesan, to garnish

Instructions

1. In a saucepan over medium-high heat, heat oil and add in garlic, onions and carrots. Allow to cook for about 2-3 minutes until beginning to brown.
2. Add tomatoes to the cooking pan along with water, spices, quinoa, bay leaves, salt and pepper. Stir well to combine, then bring the mixture to a boil.
3. Close the lid and reduce the heat to simmer. Allow to simmer for 20 minutes then remove the lid. Stir in the remaining vegetables and cook for additional 1o minutes until the asparagus has begun to soften but still has a light crunch.
4. Taste and adjust seasonings. Serve immediately garnished with nutritional yeast or cheese to get some cheesy flavor. Enjoy!

Nutritional Info (Per Serving): 119 calories; 3 g fat; 19 g total carbs; 5 g protein

Quinoa Black Bean Pumpkin Soup

Cooking Time: 25 minutes

Servings: 4

Ingredients

- 3 cups pumpkin, cubed
- 1 tablespoon olive oil
- 1 red chili pepper, diced
- 1 onion, diced
- 1/2 cup quinoa
- 5 cups vegetable broth
- 5 garlic cloves, diced
- 1/2 teaspoon red pepper flakes, crushed
- 1 teaspoon ground cumin
- 20 oz. can black beans, rinsed, drained
- 2 bay leaves
- 1/2 teaspoon dried oregano

Instructions

1. Preheat oil in a pan over medium heat, add onion. Allow onion to cook for few minutes, then add in garlic and the red chili pepper. Allow to cook until aromatic.
2. Add pumpkin to the cooking pan along with the spices. Allow to cook for a couple of minutes, add in 2 cups of vegetable broth and quinoa.
3. Bring to a boil and allow to cook for 5 minutes, then add in the remaining vegetable broth.
4. Bring to a boil again, then add in beans and the bay leaves. Bring to a boil.
5. Reduce the heat and simmer for about 5-10 minutes. Serve and garnish with cilantro, lime juice and avocado. Enjoy!

Nutritional Info (Per Serving): 384 calories; 12 g fat; 57 g total carbs; 14 g protein

Turmeric Lentil Soup

Cooking Time: 30 minutes   **Servings:** 4

Ingredients

- 1 cup carrots, grated
- 2 tablespoons olive oil
- 1½ teaspoons turmeric
- 1 small onion, grated
- ½ teaspoon cumin
- 5 cups vegetable broth
- 1 small zucchini, grated
- 1½ teaspoons salt
- ½ cup quick cook faro
- 1 cup kale, chopped, stems removed
- ½ cup red lentils
- ¼ teaspoon pepper

Instructions

1. Heat oil in a cooking pot over medium-high heat, then add in onion, carrots and zucchini. Allow to cook for about 1-2 minutes, add salt, turmeric, pepper and cumin. Allow to cook for additional 2-3 minutes until you start to smell the spices toasting.
2. Stir the broth in the cooking pot. Bring to a boil. Add in farro and lentils once boiling and simmer over low heat until the lentils and farro are well cooked, about 20 minutes.
3. Add chopped kale during last couple of minutes and stir well until wilted. Serve immediately topped with bread croutons and enjoy!

Nutritional Info (Per Serving): 207 calories; 7.5 g fat; 30 g total carbs; 7 g protein

Miso, Lentil, and Pumpkin Soup

Cooking Time: 35 minutes   **Servings:** 4

Ingredients

- 3 tablespoons olive oil
- 3 lbs. pumpkin, seeded, peeled and chopped
- 1 cinnamon stick
- 2 carrots, coarsely chopped
- 1 inch piece ginger, thinly sliced
- 1 onion, diced
- 1/3 cup lentils or split peas
- 1 garlic, finely chopped
- 1 ½ teaspoon cumin seeds
- 1 chili, chopped
- 3 tablespoons white miso paste

Instructions

1. Preheat oil in a pan over low heat, add in onion, garlic and salt. Allow to cook as you stir occasionally until garlic and onion are soft, about 3 minutes.
2. Add carrots to the cooking pan along with the pumpkin and split peas. Stir well to coat in the onion mixture, then add in about 6 cups of water. Bring to a boil.
3. Simmer until the spilt peas have become soft, about 30 minutes, then remove and discard the cinnamon stick from the soup.
4. Blend the soup until smooth, allow it to cool. Stir miso paste slowly in the cooled soup.
5. Serve soup warm and top with the sprouts, roasted seeds and anise. Enjoy!

Nutritional Info (Per Serving): 283 calories; 11.7 g fat; 41 g total carbs; 9 g protein

Green Pozole With Chickpeas

Cooking Time: 20 minutes

Servings: 4

Ingredients

For the Soup:
- 2 cups water
- 10 tomatillos, tomato, peeled and washed
- 1 ½ cups chickpeas, cooked
- ¼ onion, sliced
- 1 teaspoon salt
- 4 garlic cloves
- 1 whole serrano chile
- 1 cup cilantro, chopped

To Serve:
- 1 avocado, cubed
- 2-3 leaves romaine lettuce, sliced
- Dry oregano
- 4 radishes, sliced
- Pumpkin seeds, to taste
- 1/4 cup cilantro, chopped
- Corn chips, baked or fried

Instructions

1. Add tomatillos in a large pot along with onion, cilantro, garlic and water. Close the lid and simmer until the tomatillos are cooked through. Make sure the cooked tomatillos are light green and very soft.
2. Process vegetables with salt in a blender or a food processor, then add blended vegetables to the cooking pot. Add in chickpeas and serrano chile.
3. Lower the heat. Test the broth and add water if it's too thick.
4. Serve soup with lettuce, oregano, cilantro, radish, pumpkin seeds, corn chips and avocado. Enjoy!

Nutritional Info (Per Serving): 449 calories; 13.3 g fat; 69 g total carbs; 22 g protein

Onion, Fennel, and Green

Lentil Soup

Cooking Time: 20 minutes   **Servings:** 4

Ingredients

For Caramelized Onions:
- ¼ cup olive oil, extra virgin
- 4 onions
- Sea salt, to taste
- ¼ cup dry white wine
  For Soup:
- 8 cups water
- 4 onions
- 2 garlic cloves, minced
- 2 tablespoons extra virgin olive oil
- 2 tablespoons dry white wine
- 1 tablespoon fresh tarragon leaves
- 1 ½ cup French green lentils
- 1 tablespoon Sherry vinegar
- 2 sprigs plus 2 tablespoons fresh thyme
- 1 tablespoon lemon juice, freshly squeezed
- 1 bay leaf
- 1 cup fennel stalks
- 1 tablespoon plus 1 teaspoon sea salt, or to taste
- 1/2 teaspoon black pepper
- 3 vegetable bouillon cubes, salt-free

Instructions

1. Prepare caramelized onions:
2. Slice onions thinly into half circles. Add the onion slices to a pan and cook them over medium heat as you stir occasionally for about 20 minutes.
3. Add ¼ cup of olive oil to the pan with onions and deglaze the pan.
4. Turn the heat to medium-low and cook for additional 20 minutes as you stir from time to time.
5. Prepare the soup:
6. Add 1 tablespoon of wine and deglaze the pan. Let rest for 10 minutes, then add 2 more tablespoons of wine. Allow to cook for another 10 minutes, add in 1 tablespoon of wine. Deglaze the pan and turn the heat off.
7. Combine lentils together with water, bay leaf and two sprigs of thyme in a large soup pot, bring to a boil. Turn the heat to medium low and cook for about 15-20 minutes. Remove the bay leaf and thyme sprigs from the pot.
8. In the meantime, cut the fennel bulb into thin slices. Add 2 tablespoons of olive oil in a pan over medium-low heat. Add in fennel stalks and garlic and sauté until garlic begins to turn golden.
9. Add tarragon to the sauté pan with fennel stalks along with 2 tablespoons of thyme and the bouillon cubes. Mash bouillon and stir everything together. Add in 1 tablespoon of wine and deglaze the pan. Stir the stalks until they begin to get sticky and turn golden.
10. Add the remaining tablespoon of wine to the sauté pan and deglaze, cook for couple of minutes. Add everything into the pan with lentils, then add 1 tablespoon of water to the pan and add to the lentils.
11. Add onions to the lentils and add 1 tablespoon of water to the pan with onions. Finally, add lemon juice, salt, sherry vinegar and pepper. Cook until it is hot and all the flavors have combined.
12. Serve with the toasted bread. Enjoy!

Nutritional Info (Per Serving): 332 calories; 18.9 g fat; 37 g total carbs; 8 g protein

Tofu Bacon Avocado Salad

Cooking Time: 15 minutes   **Servings:** 4

Ingredients

- 1 avocado, sliced
- 1 head romaine lettuce, washed, chopped
- 12 slices tofu bacon , cut into bite sized pieces
- 1 can black beans, drained
- 24 cherry tomatoes
- 1 red onion, diced
- 1 can corn
- ½ cup cilantro, chopped
- Lime wedges, for serving
- Tortilla strips, for serving

Instructions

1. Divide all the ingredients amonf plates. Layer the lettuce on the bottom, then add corn and beans, followed by tofu and tomatoes.
2. Arrange avocado slices on top and sprinkle with cilantro and onions.
3. Add some tortilla chips and serve. Sprinkle with oil and top with lemon wedges.

Nutritional Info (Per Serving): 334 calories; 11.9 g fat; 47.2 g total carbs; 17.7 g protein

Peanut Noodle Salad

Cooking Time: 5 minutes　　　　　　　　　　　**Servings:** 4

Ingredients

- 2 scallions, chopped
- 8 oz. rice noodles, or substitute with linguini or spaghetti pasta
- 1/3 cup peanuts, chopped
- 1/2 red bell pepper, sliced
- 1/2 teaspoon black sesame seeds
- 1 cup carrots, shredded
- For the Peanut Dressing:
- 1 tablespoon rice vinegar
- 1/3 cup peanut butter, crunchy
- 2 tablespoons hot water
- 2 garlic cloves, minced
- 3 tablespoons sriracha

Instructions

1. Cook noodles according to the package directions, then drain and rinse with cold water in a colander until cool. Set the noodles aside.
2. In a mixing bowl, combine all the ingredients for the peanut dressing and mix until smooth. Set the mixture aside.
3. Combine noodles with peanut dressing and all other ingredients, then toss and mix well.
4. Store in the refrigerator until when ready to serve. Enjoy!

Nutritional Info (Per Serving): 267 calories; 12.3 g fat; 32 g total carbs; 9 g protein

Greek Power Salad

Cooking Time: 20 minutes	**Servings:** 4

Ingredients

- 1 cup cherry tomatoes, halved
- ¾ cup red quinoa, uncooked
- ⅓ cup almonds, toasted
- 1 cup cucumber, chopped
- ½ cup kalamata olives, halved
- 4 cups mild greens
- For Lemon Oregano Vinaigrette:
- 1 garlic clove
- ⅓ cup olive oil, extra virgin
- ⅛ teaspoon sea salt
- 2 tablespoons lemon juice
- 1 heaping tablespoon fresh oregano leaves
- 2 tablespoons white wine vinegar
- 1 tablespoon, plus 1 teaspoon maple syrup
- ⅛ teaspoon black pepper
- ½ teaspoons Dijon mustard

Instructions

1. Rinse quinoa. Mix rinsed quinoa with 1 ½ cups of water in a saucepan, bring to a boil. Close the lid and lower the heat to a simmer. Allow to cook for 15 minutes.
2. Turn the heat off after 15 minutes and allow the quinoa to steam with the lid on for additional 5 minutes.
3. Rinse quinoa under cold water.
4. Assemble the salad. Combine all the salad ingredients and toss them with lemon oregano vinaigrette. Serve and enjoy!

Nutritional Info (Per Serving): 341 calories; 21.9 g fat; 32 g total carbs; 16 g protein

Mushroom, Lemon and Lentil Salad

Cooking Time: 40 minutes

Servings: 2

Ingredients

- 2 teaspoons olive oil
- 1/2 cup French green lentils
- 1 ½ tablespoons lemon juice
- 2 cups vegetable stock or water
- 3 teaspoon olive oil
- 4 cups button and Swiss brown mushrooms mixture, sliced
- Sea salt and pepper, to taste
- 1/2 shallot or small onion, chopped
- 1/2 cup arugula
- 2 tablespoons flat leaf parsley, chopped
- 2 garlic cloves, chopped
- 1/4 teaspoon chilli flakes

Instructions

1. Cook lentils. Add lentils and vegetable stock to a saucepan and bring to a boil. Reduce the heat to a simmer and cook until the lentils are tender, about 25 minutes. Drain the lentils and set aside to cool.
2. Heat a frying pan over high heat until hot, add 1/3 of the mushrooms. Allow the mushrooms to cook for about 2 minutes, stir while cooking. Cook the mushrooms for additional 1 minute then remove them from the pan. Repeat the cooking process with the remaining mushrooms.
3. Turn the heat to medium-low, add 2 teaspoons of olive oil or vegan butter to the cooking pan. Add in shallot or onion and cook until the edges are slightly golden. Add the mushrooms back to the pan and add garlic and chilli flakes. Cook until garlic is fragrant but not browned, for about 2 minutes. Set aside to cool.
4. Toss mushroom, lentils and garlic together with lemon juice and extra virgin olive oil, then season well to taste. Add parsley and rocket as you are serving and enjoy!

Nutritional Info (Per Serving): 122 calories; 7 g fat; 14 g total carbs; 3 g protein

Dinner

Tomato-Braised Lentils

Cooking Time: 40 minutes   **Servings:** 4

Ingredients

- 1 garlic clove, sliced
- 4 tablespoons extra virgin olive oil
- 1 bunch broccoli rabe
- 1 onion, chopped
- 1 tomato, chopped
- 1 garlic clove, minced
- 1/2 cup coconut cream
- 1 ½ cups green French lentils
- 2 tablespoons plant based butter
- 1 tablespoon tomato paste
- 3 cups vegetable stock
- Salt and pepper, to taste
- 1 handful fresh basil leaves, torn

Instructions

1. Heat 2 tablespoons of olive oil in a saucepan over low heat, and add in onions. Cook the onions until translucent, season with salt and pepper.
2. Add minced garlic to the pan and cook for 1 minute, then add in lentils, tomato paste and a splash of stock.
3. Turn the heat to medium and cook as you stir occasionally until the stock is absorbed. Add stock bit by bit as you stir occasionally for about 30 minutes until the lentils are tender.
4. In the meantime, prepare a large ice bath and bring another pot of water to boil. Add broccoli rabe into the pot with boiling water and cook for 1-2 minutes. Remove the broccoli rabe and place into the ice bath.
5. Drain the cooled broccoli rabe and pat it dry. Heat the remaining 2 tablespoons of olive oil in a separate skillet or a pan, then add in broccoli rabe and sliced garlic clove. Season with salt and pepper and sauté for about 2-3 minutes.
6. Add chopped tomato to lentils and cook for 2-3 minutes, then add in cream and butter. Stir in basil leaves and serve immediately. Enjoy with sautéed broccoli rabe on top.

Nutritional Info (Per Serving): 638 calories; 32.6 g fat; 63.2 g total carbs; 28.6 g protein

Caesar White Bean Burgers

Cooking Time: 20 minutes

Servings: 4

Ingredients

- 2 garlic cloves, minced
- 2 tablespoons olive oil
- 1 flax egg
- ½ onion, diced
- 3 tablespoons lemon juice
- 2 (14 oz.) cans white beans, drained and rinsed
- ¼ teaspoon salt
- ½ cup breadcrumbs
- 2 teaspoons Dijon mustard
- 2 teaspoons Worcestershire sauce
- ¼ cup fresh parsley leaves, chopped
- 4 hamburger buns
- ¼ teaspoon ground black pepper

Instructions

1. Heat 1 tablespoon of oil in a skillet until shimmering, then add in onion. Cook the onions as you stir occasionally for about 5 minutes until softened. Add garlic and allow to cook for additional 1 minute, then remove the pan from heat.
2. Mash beans with a fork in a bowl. Add onion to the mashed beans, add breadcrumbs, parsley, lemon juice, flax egg, mustard, salt, Worcestershire sauce and pepper and mix well until combined. Cover the bowl and refrigerate for 1-2 hours.
3. Divide the mixture into 4 portions. Shape each portion into ½ inch thick patty.
4. Heat 1 tablespoon of oil in a frying pan over medium heat until shimmering, then add the patties. Cook for about 5-6 minutes until golden brown, then flip and continue cooking for another 5-6 minutes on the other side.
5. Place the cooked burgers on top of buns and add your desired toppings. Serve and enjoy!

Nutritional Info (Per Serving): 533 calories; 13.7 g fat; 76.8 g total carbs; 26.7 g protein

Quinoa Stuffed Peppers

Cooking Time: 1 hour 20 minutes   **Servings:** 8

Ingredients

- 2 garlic cloves, chopped
- 1 tablespoon olive oil
- 1 ½ teaspoons ground cumin
- 1 onion, diced
- 1 teaspoon salt
- 1 cup quinoa, rinsed
- 8 bell peppers
- 2 tablespoons tomato paste
- 1 (15 oz.) can black beans, drained and rinsed
- 1 ½ teaspoons chili powder
- 1 ½ cups corn kernels, fresh or frozen
- 2 cups water
- Freshly ground black pepper
- 1/2 cup fresh cilantro, chopped

Instructions

1. Preheat the oven to 375 F. Pour water into the baking dish just enough to cover the bottom of a baking dish and set aside.
2. Heat a tablespoon of oil in a saucepan over medium heat until shimmering and add onion. Season with salt and cook for about 8 minutes as you stir occasionally until the onions are softened.
3. Add quinoa to the saucepan with onions and cook for about 2 minutes as you stir occasionally.
4. Add tomato paste to the cooking saucepan along with garlic, chili powder and cumin. Cook for about 2 minutes as you stir occasionally until fragrant.
5. Add 2 cups of water and a teaspoon of salt to the saucepan and season with pepper. Stir well to combine.
6. Bring to a boil, reduce the heat to lowest setting. Cover the saucepan with a tight-fitting lid and cook for 15 minutes undisturbed.
7. In the meantime, prepare the bell peppers. Remove tops from peppers, remove the core. Drizzle with about ½ teaspoon of oil and season generously with salt and pepper. Set the bell peppers aside.
8. Remove quinoa from heat when ready. Allow the quinoa to stand covered for 5 minutes, fluff it gently with a fork. Add beans, corn and cilantro to the pan with quinoa and stir well to combine. Taste and adjust on salt and pepper.
9. Divide the mixture evenly among the peppers and top with caps. Place stuffed peppers into the prepared baking dish in a single layer.
10. Cover tightly with aluminum foil and bake for about 1 hour. Uncover and let rest for 5 minutes. Enjoy!

Nutritional Info (Per Serving): 248 calories; 4.3 g fat; 43.7 g total carbs; 9.6 g protein

Tofu Chickpea Stir-Fry

Cooking Time: 20 minutes

Servings: 4

Ingredients

For the sauce:
- 2 tablespoons rice vinegar
- 1/3 cup water
- 2 teaspoons maple syrup
- ¼ cup tahini
- 1 teaspoon fresh ginger, minced
- 2 tablespoons tamari or soy sauce

For the stir fry:
- ½ red onion, thinly sliced
- 1 tablespoon peanut oil
- 1 bell pepper, cored, seeded, diced
- 1 cup chickpeas, cooked or canned
- 8 oz. baked tofu, cubed
- 2 teaspoons fresh ginger, chopped

Instructions

1. Prepare the sauce by stirring together the sauce ingredients in a bowl.
2. Prepare the stir-fry. Heat oil in a skillet or wok over medium-high heat until shimmering, add in chickpeas as you stir, for about 2 minutes.
3. Stir the minced ginger into the skillet and cook for additional 1 minute. Add onion and peppers to the skillet and cook for about 2-3 minutes until the onions are tender.
4. Toss the baked tofu into the skillet and cook for about 4-6 minutes as you stir until the tofu is golden and chickpeas are browning. Pour tahini sauce over the tofu and cook for 1 minute more until the sauce has heated through.
5. Serve and enjoy topped with toasted sesame seeds and minced chives.

Nutritional Info (Per Serving): 438 calories; 15.4 g fat; 61 g total carbs; 15.7 g protein

Smoky Tempeh Burrito Bowls

Cooking Time: 30 minutes   **Servings:** 3-4

Ingredients

- 1/2 teaspoon cumin powder
- 1 (15 oz.) can black beans
- 1 cup brown rice, cooked
- For Tempeh:
- 1 tablespoon olive oil
- 10 oz. tempeh, cubed
- For Marinade:
- 2 garlic cloves, minced
- 1 tablespoon olive oil
- 1/2 white onion, diced
- 1 whole chipotle in adobo sauce, canned plus 1 tablespoon sauce
- 1 (15 oz.) can tomato sauce

Instructions

1. Steam the tempeh. Add 1 inch of water to a saucepan and bring to a simmer. Insert a steamer basket and add tempeh. Cover and steam for 15 minutes. Cube the tempeh once steamed and set aside.
2. Prepare the sauce. Heat a skillet over medium heat until hot, then add oil and onion. Cook as you stir frequently for about 3 minutes until soft and slightly browned.
3. Add garlic to the skillet and cook for additional 1-2 minutes. Add tomato sauce to the skillet along with chipotle pepper and adobo sauce. Stir and heat until bubbly.
4. Reduce the heat to low and simmer for 3-4 minutes, then transfer the sauce to a blender. Blend on high until the sauce is completely smooth.
5. Return the sauce to the skillet and turn the heat to low. Allow the sauce to cook as you stir occasionally until it has thickened.
6. Add black beans to a saucepan and heat over medium heat until bubbling. Reduce the heat and add in cumin and a pinch of sea salt. Stir and reduce the heat to low. Mash the beans with a wooden spoon (optional).
7. Heat a separate skillet over medium heat until hot. Add oil and the steamed tempeh, cook for about 6-8 minutes until crisp and brown on all sides. Add tempeh to the red sauce and stir gently to coat well.
8. Cover and let rest for about 2-3 minutes. Divide the beans, rice, vegetables of choice and tempeh between the serving bowls, and garnish with lime and fresh cilantro. Enjoy!

Nutritional Info (Per Serving): 602 calories; 21.8 g fat; 79 g total carbs; 28.7 g protein

Sweet and Sour Tempeh

Cooking Time: 20 to 30 minutes   **Servings:** 2

Ingredients

For Stir-Fry:
- 1 tablespoon sunflower oil
- 1/2 bell pepper, cut into chunks or slices
- 1 packet gluten-free tempeh, cut into squares
- Large handful snow peas
- 1 brown onion, diced
- 1 teaspoon sesame oil
  For Sweet and Sour Sauce:
- 1 tablespoon ketchup
- 2 teaspoons cornstarch dissolved in 4 teaspoons of water
- 1/3 cup rice vinegar
- 1 teaspoon tamari
- ¼ cup coconut sugar

Instructions

1. Add all ingredients for the sauce to a saucepan and turn the heat on. Bring everything to a boil, then turn off the heat. Add cornstarch mixture slowly and gradually, stirring constantly until thickened. Set aside.
2. Preheat sesame and sunflower oil in a pan over medium-high heat. Fry tempeh until all sides are browned.
3. Add diced onion and fry until browned, for 2 to 3 minutes. Add in prepped veggies and cook for a few minutes.
4. Pour in prepared sweet and sour sauce and cook for 1 to 2 minutes.
5. Serve over brown rice and top with chunks of pineapple and sesame seeds, if desired.

Nutritional Info (Per Serving): 491 calories; 12 g fat; 52 g total carbs; 24 g protein

Korean Braised Tofu

Cooking Time: 15 minutes   **Servings:** 4

Ingredients

- 1/2-1 tablespoon Korean chili powder
- Toasted sesame seeds (optional)
- 1 onion, cut into thin slices
- 1 scallion, cut into thin slices
- 1 (14-oz.) block firm tofu, cut into 16 squares
- 4 tablespoons sake
- 1 tablespoon sugar
- 3 tablespoons soy sauce

Instructions

1. Add slices of onion into a frying pan/nonstick skillet and top with tofu slices.
2. Combine together 3 tablespoons soy sauce, 1 tablespoon sugar, 4 tablespoons sake and 1/2-1 tablespoon Korean chili powder. Pour over tofu and cover the pan.
3. Raise the heat and cook everything until boiling.
4. Now reduce the heat to medium and cook for 4 to 5 minutes.
5. Uncover the pan and raise the heat again. Cook until sauce has been reduced.
6. Remove from heat and transfer Korean braised tofu to a serving platter.
7. Garnish with sesame seeds and scallions and enjoy!

Nutritional Info (Per Serving): 226 calories; 12 g fat; 11 g total carbs; 19 g protein

Red Lentil Tikka Masala

Cooking Time: 30 minutes   **Servings:** 24 to 5

Ingredients

- 1 1/2 tablespoons garam masala
- Salt and pepper, to taste
- 2 tablespoons olive oil
- 1/4 cup cilantro, chopped
- 1 onion, diced
- 1/2 cup coconut milk
- 1 small Serrano or jalapeño pepper, minced
- 1 cup red lentils
- 1 tablespoon ginger, grated
- 1 1/2 cups vegetable broth
- 3 garlic cloves, minced
- 1 tablespoon coconut sugar
- 1 tablespoon tomato paste
- 1 (28-oz.) can crushed tomatoes

Instructions

1. Preheat olive oil in a pan over medium heat and sauté Serrano pepper and onion for few minutes, until softened.
2. Add in 1 tablespoon tomato paste, 1 1/2 tablespoons garam masala, 1 tablespoon ginger, and 3 minced cloves of garlic. Stir for a minute, until fragrant.
3. Now add in 1 1/2 cups vegetable broth, 1 tablespoon coconut sugar and can crushed tomatoes. Stir well until combined, then add 1 cup red lentils.
4. Turn the heat down and simmer covered for 25 to 30 minutes, until lentils are tender.
5. Stir in 1/4 cup chopped cilantro and 1/2 cup coconut milk. Serve and enjoy!

Nutritional Info (Per Serving): 708 calories; 15 g fat; 56 g total carbs; 30 g protein

Thai Red Tofu Curry

Cooking Time: 30 minutes	**Servings:** 3 to 5

Ingredients

For the Tofu and Marinade:
- 2 tablespoons sesame oil
- 3 tablespoons corn starch
- 16-oz. extra firm tofu, drained, pressed and cut into cubes
- 1 teaspoon red pepper flakes
- 1 garlic clove, minced
- 3 tablespoons rice vinegar
- 3 tablespoons soy sauce or tamari
- 1 tablespoon brown sugar

For the Curry:
- 3 tablespoons red curry paste
- 1 small yellow onion, minced
- 8 fresh Thai basil leaves, ribboned
- 3 large cloves garlic, minced
- 1 lime, juice and zest
- 1 teaspoon of ginger, grated
- 1 tablespoon hot chili paste (sambal oelek)
- 1 red bell pepper, sliced
- 1 tablespoon soy sauce or tamari
- 1 cup Cremini mushrooms, sliced
- 13 oz. light coconut milk
-

Instructions

1. To Make the Tofu:
2. Add 3 tablespoons soy sauce or tamari, 2 tablespoons sesame oil, 1 tablespoon brown sugar, 1 teaspoon red pepper flakes, garlic, and 3 tablespoons rice vinegar to a bowl. Mix well.
3. Add tofu cubes to a freezer bag and pour in marinade. Shake well until coated and marinade for at least half an hour or up to 1 day. Transfer to a bowl and add in 3 tablespoons of corn starch. Toss well.
4. Preheat coconut oil in a pan over medium-high heat and fry each side of tofu cubes for approximately 2 minutes, until crispy and golden brown. Once done, transfer to a bowl.
5. To Make the Curry:
6. Simmer ¼ cup of water in a saucepan. Add garlic, a teaspoon of grated ginger, and minced onion.
7. Simmer until onions are translucent, for about 5 minutes over medium heat.
8. Add mushrooms, red pepper slices and 3 tablespoons of red curry paste. Stir well until all veggies are coated.
9. Now add 1 tablespoon soy sauce or tamari, 13 oz. light coconut milk, lime zest and juice.
10. Stir well and let the curry simmer for about 15 minutes.
11. Meanwhile, prepare rice as per directions mentioned on the package. Once done, transfer to a serving bowl and spoon curry on top followed by crispy tofu, sliced scallions and Thai basil ribbons.

Nutritional Info (Per Serving): 602 calories; 21.8 g fat; 79 g total carbs; 28.7 g protein

Barbecue Baked Seitan Strips

Cooking Time: 1 hour

Servings: 4 to 8

Ingredients

For the Dough:
- 1/2 teaspoon dried oregano
- 1 tablespoon soy sauce
- 3 cups vital wheat gluten
- 2 tablespoons olive oil
- 1/2 cup nutritional yeast
- 2 tablespoons maple syrup
- 1 1/2 tablespoons garlic powder
- 1 1/2 cups vegetable broth
- 1 teaspoon smoked paprika
- 1 cup vegan barbecue sauce, store bought or homemade
- 1 teaspoon onion powder
- 1/2 teaspoon dried basil
- 1/2 teaspoon ground black pepper

For the Marinade:
- 2 tablespoons soy sauce
- 1/2 teaspoons paprika
- 2 cups vegetable broth
- 1 teaspoon garlic powder
- 1 cup vegan barbecue sauce, store bought or homemade
- 1 teaspoon ground black pepper
- 3 tablespoons maple syrup
- 1 teaspoon liquid smoke
- 3 tablespoons olive oil
- 2 teaspoons hot sauce (optional)

Instructions

1. To a bowl, add 1/2 teaspoon dried basil, 3 cups vital wheat gluten, 1/2 teaspoon dried oregano, 1/2 cup nutritional yeast, 1 teaspoon smoked paprika, 1/2 teaspoon ground black pepper, 1 1/2 tablespoons garlic powder, and 1 teaspoon onion powder. Mix well.
2. Take another bowl and combine together 1 1/2 cups vegetable broth, 1 cup vegan barbecue sauce, 2 tablespoons maple syrup, 1 tablespoon soy sauce and 2 tablespoons olive oil. Pour this mixture over dry ingredients and mix with your hands. Knead for a few minutes. Add more broth if needed.
3. Add all the marinade ingredients to a bowl and mix well until combined. Place dough onto a flat surface and slightly flatten with your hands.
4. Spread a bit of olive oil on top of dough to prevent sticking. Then roll out the dough into 9x12-inch rectangular shape 1/2-1 inch thick.
5. Add a cup of marinade to a roasting dish and lay rolled out dough on top. Pour remaining marinade over dough and bake in a reheated oven at 390°F, for about an hour.
6. After half an hour, add one more cup of broth if it's too dry. Once done, serve right away and enjoy!

Nutrition Info (per serving): 286 calories; 22 g fat; 14 g total carbs; 19 g protein

Teriyaki Glazed Tofu Steaks

Cooking Time: 15 minutes

Servings: 2 to 3

Ingredients

For the Teriyaki Sauce:
- 2 tablespoons maple syrup
- 1/4 teaspoon corn starch
- 1/2 teaspoon ginger, grated
- 1/4 teaspoon Dijon mustard
- 1 teaspoon minced garlic
- 1 tablespoon apple cider vinegar or rice vinegar
- 1 tablespoon lemon juice
- 4 tablespoons soy sauce

For the Tofu Steaks:
- Oil, for coating the pan
- 1 (14-oz.) block extra firm tofu, cut into 1/2-inch thick slices

Instructions

1. Add all the teriyaki sauce ingredients to a bowl and mix well. Coat a skillet-pan with oil and warm it up.
2. Add tofu steaks to a pan in batches and cook until both sides are covered with golden-brown crust.
3. Pour in half or the prepared sauce when one batch is done and cook for about 2 minutes, until the sauce thickens.
4. Cook remaining tofu in a similar way. Serve immediately!

Nutrition Info (per serving): 239 calories; 15.4 g fat; 4 g total carbs; 21 g protein

Chilli Sin Carne

Cooking Time: 30 minutes

Servings: 6

Ingredients

- 1 teaspoon ground cumin
- 1 cup vegetable stock
- 2 tablespoons olive oil
- 1 lb frozen soy mince
- 3 garlic cloves, minced
- 3 ½ oz split red lentils
- 1 red onion, thinly sliced
- 1 tin (14 oz) red kidney beans, drained and rinsed
- 2 celery stalks, chopped
- 28 oz tinned chopped tomatoes
- 2 carrots, peeled and chopped
- 2 red peppers, chopped
- 1 teaspoon chili powder
- Salt and pepper, to taste

Instructions

1. Add oil to a pan and preheat over medium-high heat.
2. Sauté peppers, celery, garlic, carrots and onion until softened, for few minutes.
3. Stir in pepper, salt, and a teaspoon of each chili powder and cumin.
4. Add in red lentils, vegetable stock, chopped tomatoes, red kidney beans and frozen soy mince. Simmer everything for approximately 25 minutes.
5. Serve with steamed basmati rice, and some fresh torn coriander. Finish with a drizzle of lime juice. Enjoy!

Nutritional Info (Per Serving): 340 calories; 18 g fat; 42 g total carbs; 25 g protein

Teriyaki Tofu Stir Fry

Cooking Time: 20 minutes   **Servings:** 4

Ingredients

- 1 tablespoon tamari or soy sauce
- 2 teaspoons cooking oil
- 14 oz. firm tofu, cut block into half, pressed
- 2 teaspoons red chili sauce (optional)
- 1 lb. asparagus, trimmed and chopped
- 2 tablespoons green onions, chopped
  For the Sauce:
- 5 garlic cloves, minced
- 1/2 cup water
- 3 tablespoons tamari or soy sauce
- 2 teaspoons corn starch
- 1 tablespoon sesame oil
- 1/4 cup coconut sugar or maple syrup
- 1.5 tablespoon rice vinegar
- 1/2 tablespoons ginger, grated
  For Serving:
- 4 cups quinoa, cooked or brown rice

Instructions

1. Cut tofu into 1/2-inch cubes. Add a teaspoon of oil in pan and fry tofu cubes over medium heat. Cook until tofu is lightly brown on most sides, flipping frequently.
2. Add a bit of oil if tofu is sticking to the pan.
3. Once done, toss tofu cubes with a tablespoon of soy sauce or tamari.
4. Transfer to a bowl and set aside. Wipe the pan quickly with wet paper napkin.
5. Combine together all the ingredients for the sauce in a bowl and set aside.
6. Sauté veggies or asparagus in a wiped pan along with a teaspoon of oil, until crispy. Transfer to fried tofu.
7. Now, add in sauce and cook until sauce begins to thicken.
8. Add more coconut sugar or tamari, if desired.
9. Stir in green onions and red chili paste. Turn off the heat and serve over cooked quinoa or rice.

Nutritional Info (Per Serving): 411 calories; 11 g fat; 58 g total carbs; 19 g protein

Farro Protein Bowl

Cooking Time: 30 minutes

Servings: 2 to 4

Ingredients

- 1 1/4 cups water
- 4 lemon wedges
- 1 cup sweet potatoes, diced
- 2 tablespoons roasted almonds
- 1 cup carrots, diced
- 1/4 cup hummus
- 2 teaspoons oil
- 2 cups mixed greens
- 15 oz. can chickpeas, drained and rinsed
- Salt and pepper, to taste
- 4 oz. smoky tempeh strips
- 1/2 cup farro, uncooked

Instructions

1. Toss carrots and potatoes with a pinch of each pepper, salt and a teaspoon of oil. Spread out on a third of the baking sheet, in a single layer.
2. Now toss chickpeas with 2 pinches of each pepper, salt and a teaspoon of oil, until coated. Spread out on second third of the baking sheet, in a single layer
3. Place strips of tempeh on the remaining third of the sheet. Roast in a preheated oven at 375F, for half an hour.
4. Flip over the strips of tempeh and stir chickpeas and potatoes (while keeping them separate).
5. Meanwhile, add 1 1/4 cups water to a pot along with hefty pinch of salt and faro grains. Cover and bring everything to a boil. Then turn the heat down and cook until grains are chewy, for about 25 to 30 minutes.
6. Once done, divide greens and faro among 2 bowls.
7. When tempeh, chickpeas and potatoes are done, sprinkle with salt if needed and divide among the bowls. Top with lime wedges, almonds and hummus. Serve and enjoy!

Nutrition Info (per serving): 590 calories; 17.8 g fat; 92 g total carbs; 18 g protein

Mongolian Seitan

Cooking Time: 20 minutes   **Servings:** 6

Ingredients

For the Sauce:
- 1/3 teaspoon red pepper flakes
- 2 tablespoons cold water
- 2 teaspoons vegetable oil
- 2 teaspoons cornstarch
- 1/2 teaspoons ginger, minced or grated
- 1/2 cup + 2 tablespoons coconut sugar
- 3 cloves garlic, minced or grated
- 1/2 cup low-sodium soy sauce
- 1/3 teaspoon Chinese five spice (optional)

For the Seitan:
- 1 lb. homemade or store bought seitan, cut into 1-inch pieces
- 1 and 1/2 tablespoon vegetable oil

Instructions

To make the sauce:

1. Preheat oil in a pan and sauté garlic and ginger for 30 seconds, stirring constantly. Then add 1/3 teaspoon Chinese five spice (if using) and 1/3 teaspoon red pepper flakes. Cook until fragrant, for about 40 to 60 seconds.
2. Stir in 1/2 cup low-sodium soy sauce and 1/2 cup + 2 tablespoons coconut sugar. Turn the heat down and simmer for 5 to 7 minutes, until sugar is completely dissolved, stirring occasionally.
3. Whisk cornstarch in cold water and stir in pan slowly and gradually. Cook until sauce has thickened, for a few minutes. Turn the heat down and simmer until ready to add to seitan.

To make the seitan:

4. Preheat oil in a skillet over medium-high heat. Cook seitan until crisped and slightly browned, for 4 to 5 minutes.
5. Turn down the heat and add in sauce. Stir well until all seitan pieces are coated with sauce.
6. Serve along with your favorite veggies and/or rice, and garnish with scallions and toasted sesame seeds, if needed.

Nutritional Info (Per Serving): 324 calories; 8 g fat; 33 g total carbs; 29 g protein

Black Bean and Quinoa Balls

Cooking Time: 1 hour   **Servings:** 4

Ingredients

- 4 zucchinis, spiralized
- Salt and pepper, to taste
- 2 tablespoons tomato paste
- ½ cup quinoa
- 1.5 tablespoon chopped fresh herbs (oregano, rosemary, sage, basil)
- 1 can black beans
- 1 teaspoon garlic powder
- ¼ cup sesame seeds
- 2 tablespoons nutritional yeast
- ¼ cup of oat flour or bread crumbs
- ½ tablespoon Sriracha
- For the Sauce:
- 2 tablespoons toasted pine nuts
- Salt and pepper, to taste
- ½ cup cherry tomatoes, halved
- 1 teaspoon oregano
- ½ cup sun-dried tomatoes
- Handful of fresh basil
- 1 tablespoon apple cider vinegar
- 2 tablespoons nutritional yeast
- 1 garlic clove
- Fresh basil, to serve

Instructions

1. Add quinoa to a pot along with a cup of water and cook for 15 minutes. Once done, drain well and allow it to cool a bit.
2. In the meantime, mash coarsely black beans in a bowl by using a fork or masher. Add in ¼ cup of oat flour/bread crumbs, 2 tablespoons tomato paste, cooked quinoa, ¼ cup of sesame seeds, 2 tablespoons nutritional yeast, ½ tablespoon Sriracha and spices. Mix with your hands until dough is formed.
3. Now make 22 to 25 balls from dough. Place balls onto a parchment-lined baking sheet.
4. Bake for about 35 to 40 minutes at 400ºF, until crispy.
5. Meanwhile, blend all the sauce ingredients in a blender, until creamy.
6. Add zucchinis to a bowl along with cherry tomatoes and sun-dried tomato sauce. Mix well.
7. Top with baked black bean and quinoa balls (3-4 balls per serving). Garnish with fresh basil and serve right away!

Nutrition Info (per serving): 241 calories; 15 g fat; 15 g total carbs; 15 g protein

Teriyaki Tempeh Tacos

Cooking Time: 20 minutes	**Servings:** 6

Ingredients

- 6 gluten free taco shells
  For Asian Slaw:
- 1 cup red cabbage, shredded
- 3 scallions, chopped
- 1 cup green cabbage, shredded
- 1 cup carrots, grated
  For Dressing:
- 1 tablespoon maple syrup
- 1/4 teaspoon pepper
- 1/4 cup apple cider vinegar
- 1/4 teaspoon salt
- 2 tablespoon sesame oil or extra virgin olive oil
- 1 tablespoon Sriracha
- 1 tablespoon lime juice
- 1 tablespoon Dijon mustard
- 1/2 tablespoon tamari or soy sauce
-

Instructions

1. Take 8 oz. package of organic tempeh and cut into squares or triangles. Transfer to a steamer basket and steam for about 10 minutes.
2. Meanwhile, prepare marinade by whisking together 1/4 teaspoon onion powder, 3 tablespoons veggie broth, 1/2 teaspoon garlic powder and 1 tablespoon tamari or soy sauce.
3. Once tempeh is cooked, transfer to a dish and pour the marinade on top. Let it sit for about 20 minutes.
4. Preheat a tablespoon of coconut oil in a pan and sear each side of tempeh for 3 to 5 minutes, until crispy.
5. Meanwhile, prepare teriyaki sauce. For this, take a bowl and mix together 1/4 teaspoon liquid smoke, ¼ cup tamari or soy sauce, 1/2 teaspoon corn starch, 1 teaspoon sesame or olive oil, 1/2 teaspoon garlic powder, 1 teaspoon sriracha, 2 tablespoons maple syrup, and 1 teaspoon rice wine/apple cider vinegar.
6. When tempeh is cooked, add to teriyaki sauce and toss well until tempeh are coated completely.
7. Now take out the tempeh from the sauce and add back to the pan. Heat each side for 30 seconds, then turn off the heat.
8. Top with remaining sauce and let it sit for a minute.
9. Add all the dressing ingredients in a bowl and mix well. Take another bowl, and mix together all the slaw ingredients.
10. Combine both dressing and slaw ingredients together. Top tacos with slaw-dressing mixture and tempeh.

Nutritional Info (Per Serving): 216 calories; 13 g fat; 15 g total carbs; 10 g protein

Spinach Ricotta Lasagne

Cooking Time: 40 minutes

Servings: 4

Ingredients

Vegan ricotta filling:
- ½ teaspoon salt
- 1 lb firm tofu, broken into big chunks
- 5 garlic cloves
- 1 tablespoon mustard
- 2 tablespoons olive oil
- A pinch of black pepper
- 2 lemons, juiced
- A pinch of nutmeg

For the Cream Sauce:
- 3 tablespoons flour
- ½ teaspoon salt
- 3 tablespoons margarine
- 3 cups soy milk

For Tomato Sauce:
- Generous pinch salt
- ½ lb lasagne sheets
- 1 cup passata
- 1 lb frozen spinach, defrosted, drained
- 2 teaspoons dried oregano
- A pinch of black pepper

Instructions

To make vegan ricotta filling:

1. To a blender, add all the filling ingredients except for tofu and blend well until creamy and smooth. Now add in tofu chunks and blend until you obtained a crumbly filling.

To Make Creamy Sauce:

2. Add margarine to a pan and allow it to melt over medium heat. Then stir in flour until you obtained a thick paste. Whisk in salt and milk until thickened.

To Make Tomato Sauce:

3. Add passata to a bowl along with salt, pepper and oregano. Mix well.

Assemble:

4. Spread tomato sauce on the bottom of the baking dish. Add lasagne sheets on top.

5. Add filling and cream sauce. Repeat layers until all the ingredients are used.

6. Cover last layer of lasagna sheet with creamy and tomato sauce. Cook at 375 F for about 30-40 minutes.

7. Once done, serve immediately and enjoy!

Nutrition Info (per serving): 473 calories; 8 g fat; 85 g total carbs; 14 g protein

Samosa Pie

Cooking Time: 20 minutes

Servings: 4

Ingredients

- 2 cans lentils, drained and rinsed
- 2 tablespoons vegetable oil
- 2 potatoes, peeled and diced
- 1 pack filo pastry, defrosted (if frozen)
- 5 oz frozen green peas
- 1 tablespoon vegetable oil
- 1 teaspoon chili powder
- 1 onion, diced
- 1 tablespoon dried coriander
- 3 garlic cloves, minced
- 2 tablespoons curry powder
- Salt and pepper, to taste

Instructions

1. Boil water in a large pot and add potatoes. Cook until soft, then add in frozen green peas in the last minute of cooking. Drain well and mash both peas and potatoes together.
2. In the meantime, preheat oil in a pan over medium heat and sauté garlic and onion until softened.
3. Add in 2 tablespoons curry powder, 1 teaspoon chili powder and 1 tablespoon dried coriander and continue cooking for a minute further. Then add lentils along with a drop of water and cook over low heat for about 10 minutes.
4. Now add mashed potatoes and peas to a pan with soy mince and sprinkle with pepper and salt. If it's too dry, add a bit of water.
5. Transfer mixture to an oven dish and spread evenly. Now unfold filo pastry and start layering on top of potato mixture, sheet by sheet.
6. Brush each layer with some oil. Cook in a preheated oven at 350F, for about 20 minutes, until crispy and golden.
7. Serve and enjoy!

Nutrition Info (per serving): 936 calories; 47.9 g fat; 50.4 g total carbs; 91.1 g protein

Lentil Roast with Balsamic Onion Gravy

Cooking Time: 45 minutes **Servings:** 6

Ingredients

For the Lentil Loaf:
- 1 can (14 oz) cooked kidney beans, rinsed
- 5 oz rolled oats
- 1 tablespoon vegetable oil
- Black pepper, to taste
- 1 onion, minced
- 4 tablespoons nutritional yeast
- 3 garlic cloves, minced
- 2 tablespoons mixed dried herbs
- 2 portobello mushrooms, chopped
- 1 tablespoon gluten-free tamari soy sauce
- 1 carrot, grated
- 1 can (14 oz) cooked puy lentils, rinsed

For the balsamic onion gravy:
- 1 tablespoon coconut sugar or brown sugar
- 3 tablespoons gluten-free tamari soy sauce
- 2 cups vegetable stock
- 3 tablespoons balsamic vinegar
- 1 red onion, sliced
- 1 cup red wine
- 2 tablespoons vegetable oil
- 1 tablespoon arrowroot powder

Instructions

To make the lentil loaf:
1. Sauté garlic and onion in oil until soft. Then add in carrots and mushrooms and continue cooking for further 5 minutes.
2. Add remaining ingredients and mash to combine. If the mixture is too wet, add some oats, if it's too dry, then add a bit of water.
3. Transfer mixture to a greaseproof paper lined loaf tin and cook in a preheated oven at 350 F, for about 40 to 45 minutes.

To make the gravy:
4. Sauté onion in oil along with sugar for about 10 minutes. Then stir in arrowroot powder and cook for a few minutes.
5. Add in stock, tamari sauce, vinegar and wine and simmer at low until stock is reduced by half.
6. Cook until you have thick and dark gravy. Serve warm with roast vegetables and lentil loaf.

Nutrition Info (per serving): 387 calories; 28.7 g fat; 25 g total carbs; 13 g protein

Snacks

Quinoa Brittle

Cooking Time: 25 minutes

Servings: 3 to 5

Ingredients

- 2 tablespoons chia seeds
- 1/2 cup maple syrup
- 1/2 cup white quinoa, uncooked
- 2 tablespoons coconut oil
- 3/4 cup pecans, chopped
- 1 pinch sea salt (optional)
- 1/4 cup gluten-free rolled oats
- 2 tablespoons coconut sugar

Instructions

1. To a bowl, add 2 tablespoons coconut sugar, a pinch of salt, 2 tablespoons chia seeds, 1/4 cup gluten-free rolled oats, 3/4 cup chopped pecans, 1/2 cup uncooked quinoa. Mix well to combine.
2. Add 1/2 cup maple syrup to a pan along with 2 tablespoons coconut oil. Warm for few minutes over medium heat, stirring occasionally. Once combined, pour over dry ingredients and stir well until combined.
3. Arrange on a baking sheet lined with parchment paper and spread evenly by using a metal spoon.
4. Bake in a preheated oven at 325 F, for 15 minutes. Then turn around the pan to ensure even browning. Continue baking for further 10 minutes, until golden brown and crisp.
5. Once done, allow it to cool, then cut into bite-size pieces. Enjoy!

Nutritional Info (Per Serving): 157 calories; 9.6 g fat; 17.2 g total carbs; 2.9 g protein

Protein Black Bean Lime Dip

Cooking Time: 20 minutes   **Servings:** 4

Ingredients

- 1 tablespoon olive oil
- Salt and pepper, to taste
- 1 garlic cloves, grated
- 10 tablespoons water
- 1 inch fresh ginger, grated
- ½ lime, juiced
- 1 can (15.5 oz.) black beans, drained and rinsed

Instructions

1. Sauté garlic and ginger in oil over medium heat.
2. Add in beans and fry for a few minutes, adding tablespoons of water as you go.
3. Turn off the heat and add in lime juice, pepper and salt.
4. Mash until you have a smooth paste.
5. Add it to salad, potatoes, bread or enjoy simply as a high protein snack!

Nutritional Info (Per Serving): 374 calories; 14 g fat; 46 g total carbs; 15 g protein

Hemp Protein Date Bars

Cooking Time: 30 minutes

Servings: 10 to 12 bars

Ingredients

- ¼ cup hemp protein powder
- 1 to 2 tablespoons water
- ⅓ cup mixed raw seeds
- ½ teaspoon vanilla
- ½ cup unsweetened coconut, shredded
- 2 tablespoons cacao powder
- 3 tablespoons hemp seeds
- 1 cup (about 13) Medjool dates

Instructions

1. Add 3 tablespoons hemp seeds to a processor along with ¼ cup hemp protein powder, ½ cup shredded coconut, and ⅓ cup mixed raw seeds. Pulse well, and transfer to a bowl.
2. Then add ½ teaspoon vanilla, 2 tablespoons cacao powder, and a cup of dates to a bowl Add a bit of water if dates are too dry. Pulse until everything is well combined.
3. Transfer seed mixture back to a processor and pulse until fully combined.
4. Transfer mixture to a loaf pan lined with parchment paper and spread evenly and press down firmly.
5. Allow it to harden in a fridge for at least 2 hours, then cut into approximately 10 to 12 bars.

Nutritional Info (per serving): 214 calories; 10 g fat; 20 g carbohydrate; 12 g protein

Maple Candied Pecans

Cooking Time: 20 minutes   **Servings:** 2 cups

Ingredients

- 1 1/2 teaspoons ground cinnamon
- 1/8 teaspoon ground cayenne
- 2 cups raw pecan halves
- 1/2 teaspoon fine sea salt
- 1/2 cup real maple syrup

Instructions

1. Add all ingredients to a pan and toss well until everything is well combined.
2. Cook over medium, stirring occasionally, until syrup comes to a low simmer.
3. Turn the heat down and simmer until maple syrup has evaporated, for around 20 to 25 minutes, stirring often.
4. Once maple syrup is crystallized, cook pecans for further 60 seconds, stirring every 20 seconds.
5. Place parchment paper onto a flat surface and place candid pecans on top.
6. Break the clumps with a spatula and spread pecans evenly. Allow them to cool and then serve immediately!
7. Leftovers pecans can be stored for u to 2 weeks in an airtight container.

Nutritional Info (per serving): 360 calories; 21.8 g fat; 31.4 g total carbs; 14.2 g protein

Smoky Maple Tofu Sandwich

Cooking Time: 1 hour

Servings: 4

Ingredients

Caramelized Onions:
- ½ tablespoon vegan butter
- 1 tablespoon water
- 1 onion, sliced
- ¼ teaspoon salt

Marinated Smoky Maple Tofu:
- 2 tablespoons soy sauce
- ½ teaspoon liquid smoke
- 1 block extra-firm tofu, sliced
- 2 tablespoons water
- ½ tablespoon canola oil
- 2 tablespoons maple syrup
- 3 garlic cloves, minced

Smoky Maple Tofu Sandwich:
- Vegan mayo, to taste
- 4 to 8 slices tomato
- 8 slices wholegrain rye bread
- 4 leaves green leaf lettuce
- 1 ripe avocado, mashed

Instructions

Marinated Smoky Maple Tofu:
1. Pat dry tofu with a clean towel.
2. Add garlic to a food container along with liquid smoke, water, maple syrup and soy sauce. Add in tofu and allow it to marinate for 30 to 60 minutes.
3. Add half tablespoon of oil into a skillet and preheat over medium heat. Add in marinated tofu (avoid overcrowding), reserving excess marinade.
4. Cook both sides until golden. Pour in reserved marinade and cook further until all the marinade has been absorbed by tofu, stirring gently. Set aside.

Caramelized Onions:
5. Heat vegan butter in a skillet over medium heat. Sauté sliced onions along with 1/4 teaspoon of salt. Caramelize the onions, stirring occasionally. Add a tablespoon of water if onions begin to get dry.
6. Once caramelized and become golden-brown, turn off the heat. It may take 45-60 minutes.

Assembling the Tofu Sandwiches:
7. Toast the bread slices lightly and spread one slice with mashed avocado and another slice with vegan mayo and Dijon mustard.
8. Cover toasted mayo/mustard slice with a leaf of lettuce followed by 1- to tomato slices, 4 tofu slices, ¼ of caramelized onions and toasted avocado bread on top. Enjoy!

Nutritional Info (Per Serving): 494 calories; 26 g fat; 20 g total carbs; 20.6 g protein

Cookie Dough Protein Bars

Cooking Time: 5 to 10 minutes   **Servings:** 5 bars

Ingredients

- 1 oz dark chocolate
- ½ lb chickpeas, washed and drained
- 1/4 cup unsweetened almond milk
- 1 ½ tablespoons quick oats
- 2 oz smooth peanut butter
- 1 scoop vanilla protein powder
- 2 teaspoons maple syrup
- 1 tablespoon cinnamon

Instructions

1. Pulse chickpeas in a food processor, until crumbly. Add in peanut butter, 2 teaspoons maple syrup and quick oats and blend for a minute.
2. Scrape off the bottom and sides and blend further for 30 seconds.
3. Add 1/4 cup unsweetened almond milk, 1 tablespoon cinnamon, and 1 scoop vanilla protein powder. Blend until you obtained sticky dough.
4. Once done, transfer to a bowl and knead with your hands and create 5 equal bars. Melt chocolate and pour over bars.
5. Transfer to a fridge for a few hours and enjoy chilled.

Nutrition Info (per serving): 432 calories; 25.5 g fat; 7 g total carbs; 43 g protein

Roasted Spaghetti Squash

Seedss

Cooking Time: 50 minutes   **Servings:** 2

Ingredients

- 1 teaspoon maple syrup
- ⅛ teaspoon kosher salt
- ½ cup spaghetti squash seeds
- ½ teaspoon ground cinnamon
- ½ teaspoon extra-virgin olive oil
- ½ teaspoon ground cumin

Instructions

1. Add spaghetti squash seeds to a bowl and toss with ⅛ teaspoon salt, ½ teaspoon ground cinnamon, ½ teaspoon ground cumin, ½ teaspoon extra-virgin olive oil and 1 teaspoon maple syrup.
2. Spread the mixture on the parchment-lined baking sheet evenly and bake in a preheated oven at 300 F, for about 15 minutes.
3. Stir and bake further for 10 to 15 minutes, until crispy and golden. Enjoy!

Nutritional Info (Per Serving): 203 calories; 17.1 g fat; 6.4 g total carbs; 9.9 g protein

White Beans Toast

Cooking Time: 10 minutes | **Servings:** 1

Ingredients

- Dash garlic powder
- 2 tablespoons tomato, chopped
- 1 slice 100% whole wheat bread, toasted
- ½ teaspoon basil pesto
- ⅓ cup canned cannellini beans (no salt added white kidney beans), rinsed and drained

Instructions

1. Top toast with cannellini beans, ½ teaspoon basil pesto, and dash of garlic powder.
2. Top with 2 tablespoons of chopped tomatoes.

Nutritional Info (Per Serving): 212 calories; 4 g fat; 36 g total carbs; 8 g protein

Grape Tofu Smoothie

Cooking Time: 5 minutes	**Servings:** 2

Ingredients

- ½ cup grape juice, chilled
- 6 oz. light soft silken tofu
- ½ cup small ice cubes or crushed ice
- ⅔ cup frozen blueberries
- 2 tablespoons creamy peanut butter
- 1 ¼ cups vanilla-flavored almond milk, chilled

Instructions

1. Add all the ingredients to a high speed blender.
2. Blitz to combine, until smooth.
3. Pour into chilled glasses and serve!

Nutritional Info (Per Serving): 247 calories; 10.5 g fat; 30.3 g total carbs; 10.7 g protein

Peanut Butter and Apple-Cinnamon Toast

Cooking Time: 10 minutes

Servings: 1

Ingredients

- 1 slice 100% whole wheat bread, lightly toasted
- Pinch ground cinnamon
- 4 teaspoons creamy peanut butter
- ¼ apple, cored and sliced

Instructions

1. Spread butter over toast and top with apple slices.
2. Sprinkle with cinnamon and serve!

Nutritional Info (Per Serving): 252 calories; 11 g fat; 33 g total carbs; 8 g protein

Edamame with Aleppo Pepper

Cooking Time: 15 minutes

Servings: 1

Ingredients

- ⅛ teaspoon Aleppo pepper
- ½ cup edamame

Instructions

1. Steam edamame for 10-15 minutes and sprinkle with pepper.
2. Serve warm!

Nutritional Info (Per Serving): 101 calories; 3 g fat; 9.2 g total carbs; 8 g protein

Peanut Butter Banana Cream

Cooking Time: 5 minutes

Servings: 2

Ingredients

- 2 bananas, peeled, halved and frozen
- Unsweetened coconut, shredded
- ¼ cup natural peanut butter

Instructions

1. Pulse butter and bananas in a food processor, until smooth.
2. Garnish with coconut and serve right away!

Nutritional Info (Per Serving): 315 calories; 16.4 g fat; 33 g total carbs; 8.3 g protein

Cheesy High Protein Popcorn

Cooking Time: 15 minutes

Servings: 2

Ingredients

- 1/2 teaspoon curry powder
- 4 cups popped popcorn, plain
- 1 teaspoon olive oil
- 1 tablespoon soya powder
- 1/2 teaspoon onion power
- 1 tablespoon nutritional yeast
- 1/2 teaspoon salt
- 1 teaspoon spirulina powder

Instructions

1. Add popcorn to a bowl.
2. Take another bowl and combine together 1 tablespoon nutritional yeast, 1 teaspoon spirulina powder, 1 tablespoon soya powder, and all the seasonings.
3. Drizzle popcorn with oil and sprinkle with seasonings.
4. Toss well and enjoy!

Nutrition Info (per serving): 130 calories; 9.9 g fat; 8 g total carbs; 13 g protein

Mango Chia Seed Smoothie

Cooking Time: 10 minutes   **Servings:** 2

Ingredients

- 1 ½ cups unsweetened almond milk
- 2 cups frozen mango chunks
- 2 tablespoons chia seeds
- 2 medium bananas, sliced and frozen

Instructions

1. Add chia seeds to a bowl along with half cup of milk. Whisk well until combined, cover and transfer to a fridge for 10 minutes.
2. Add remaining ingredients to a high speed blender. Blitz to combine, until smooth.
3. Take out the chia seeds and whisk again. Transfer to a blender and blend until smooth and creamy.
4. Pour into chilled glasses and serve!

Nutrition Info (per serving): 396 calories; 15 g fat; 55 g total carbs; 17 g protein

Spicy Garlic Roasted Chickpeas

Cooking Time: 25 minutes   **Servings:** 6

Ingredients

- 1/2 teaspoon cumin
- 2 (15 oz.) cans chickpeas, drained
- ¼ to ½ teaspoon cayenne pepper
- ¼ cup olive oil
- ½ teaspoon onion powder
- 1 teaspoon sea salt
- ¾ teaspoon garlic powder
- 1/2 teaspoon chili powder
- ¾ teaspoon paprika
- Sea salt, to taste

Instructions

1. Air dry chickpeas to a strainer lined with paper towel and let drain for 10 to 15 minutes.
2. Then, place onto a baking sheet lined with parchment paper. Drizzle with oil and stir well until coated. Sprinkle with half of salt.
3. Transfer to a preheated oven at 425° F, and cook until golden brown for about 20 to 25 minutes, stirring every few minutes.
4. Once done, take out from the oven.
5. Combine together ¾ teaspoon paprika, 1/2 teaspoon chili powder, ¾ teaspoon garlic powder, ¼ to ½ teaspoon cayenne pepper, 1/2 teaspoon cumin, remaining half teaspoon of salt, and ½ teaspoon onion powder.
6. Toss warm chickpeas with prepared spice mixture and adjust salt, if needed. Enjoy!

Nutrition Info (per serving): 356 calories; 13 g fat; 53 g total carbs; 17 g protein

Dessert

Classic Baked Cheesecake

Cooking Time: 1 hour

Servings: 6

Ingredients

Crust:
- 1 ½ cups cashews
- 8 medjool dates, pitted and soaked in warm water
- 2 tablespoons cashew butter

Filling:
- 1 cup raw cashews, presoaked and strained
- 1 cup vanilla coconut yogurt
- 6 tablespoons agave
- 2 tablespoons lemon juice
- 1 tablespoon psyllium husk
- 1 teaspoon pure vanilla extract
- ½ teaspoon raw ground vanilla bean
- salt, to taste

Instructions

1. Preheat the oven to 350 F, grease a spring form pan with non-stick cooking oil.
2. To a food processor ad all crust ingredients and process until a fine crumbly sticky mixture is formed, transfer the mixture to the pan and press it down.
3. To a blender add all filling ingredients. Blend into a smooth mixture, add to the crust and spread in an even layer. Place in the oven and bake for 40 minutes until firm and golden.
4. Once done, remove from the oven and set aside to cool on a wire rack.
5. Once done, serve.

Nutritional information (per serving): 534 calories; 30 g fat; 58 g total carbs; 15 g protein

Blueberry Crisp

Cooking Time: 45minutes **Servings:** 10

Ingredients

- 7 cups blueberries
- 2 cups oats
- ½ cup water
- 3 tablespoons lemon juice
- 4 tablespoons lemon zest
- 1 cup maple syrup
- 1 cup almonds, chopped
- 2 tablespoons flax seed
- 4 tablespoons cinnamon
- salt, to taste

Instructions

1. Preheat the oven to 375 F.
2. To a baking dish, fill it with all the blueberries
3. Drizzle lemon juice on the berries, set aside
4. To a food processor add 1 cup oats, ½ cup almonds, flax seed, 2 tablespoons cinnamon and salt. Set aside
5. To a large bowl combine remaining oat, ½ cup almonds, 2 tablespoon lemon zest, ½ cup maple syrup, ¼ cup water and salt. Mix well
6. Drizzle remaining maple syrup over the berries
7. Sprinkle a layer of blended oat mixture on top of berries, add a layer of wet oat mixture, ¼ cup water and the remaining lemon zest and cinnamon.
8. Place in the oven and bake for 35 minutes until bubbly.
9. Once done, remove from oven and let it cool.
10. Once done, serve.

Nutritional information (per serving): 336 calories; 8 g fat; 62 g total carbs; 9 g protein

Plant Based Peanut Butter

Cream Sweet Potato Brownies

Cooking Time: 8 hours 30 minutes   **Servings:** 10

Ingredients

- 1 large sweet potato
- 8 medjool dates, pitted and soaked in warm water for ½ an hour
- ¼ cup + 3 tablespoons natural peanut butter
- ¼ cup cacao
- 8 oz. full fat coconut cream, chilled
- 4 tablespoons maple syrup
- cinnamon for dusting

Instructions

1. Place sweet potato in a microwave safe bowl, poke some holes using a fork and microwave it for 5 minutes until soft.
2. To a food processor add sweet potato, dates, ¼ cup peanut butter, 2 tablespoons maple syrup and cocoa. Blend until smooth.
3. Transfer to a muffin tin, leaving a divot in the middle of each brownie for the filling.
4. Place in the oven and bake on 325 F for ½ hour. Remove and set aside to cool.
5. Meanwhile with an electric mixer whisk cooled coconut cream, remaining peanut butter, and the remaining maple syrup until stiff.
6. Spread the filling on the cooled brownies, dust with cinnamon.
7. Place in the refrigerator to cool for 8-12 hours.
8. Once done, serve.

Nutritional information (per serving): 210 calories; 12 g fat; 26 g total carbs; 3 g protein

Raw Vegan Chickpea Cookie Dough

Cooking Time: 10 minutes

Servings: 2

Ingredients

- 1 can chickpeas, drained and rinsed
- ¼ cup vegan dark chocolate chips
- 1 tablespoon vanilla extract
- 4 or more tablespoons water
- 1 tablespoon all natural peanut butter
- 3 tablespoons maple syrup
- 1 dash sea salt

Instructions

1. To a blender add chickpeas, vanilla extract, water, peanut butter, maple syrup and salt. Blend until smooth.
2. Transfer to a glass or a serving bowl.
3. Stir in the chocolate chips.
4. Once done, serve.

Nutritional information (per serving): 320 calories; 7 g fat; 52 g total carbs; 11 g protein

Whole Food Plant Based Apple Crisp

Cooking Time: 50 minutes

Servings: 8

Ingredients

Apple base:
- 6 apples, sliced
- ¾ cup water
- 1 tablespoon lemon juice
- 2 teaspoons cinnamon
- 2 tablespoons maple syrup
- 1 pinch sea salt

Crumble:
- 1 ½ cups oats
- 1 cups walnuts
- 1 tablespoon cinnamon
- 4 tablespoons maple syrup
- 1 dash sea salt

Instructions

1. Preheat the oven to 350 F.
2. In a bowl combine the apple base ingredients excluding apples.
3. Place apples in a microwave safe dish, pour base ingredients on top and microwave on high for 5 minutes.
4. To a food processor add oats and process until a coarse flour is formed.
5. To the food processor add the remaining crumble ingredients until walnuts break, spread this mixture over microwaved apples. Bake in the oven for 40 minutes.
6. Once done, serve.

Nutritional information (per serving): 223 calories; 8 g fat; 43 g total carbs; 5 g protein

Vegan Chocolate Beet Cake

Cooking Time: 1 hour 20 minutes   **Servings:** 10

Ingredients

- ½ cup semisweet chocolate chips
- 1 cup coconut oil, melted and cooled slightly
- 2 cups canned beets
- 1 cup sugar
- 2 cups all-purpose flour
- 3 flax eggs
- 2 teaspoon baking soda
- 2 teaspoon vanilla
- ¼ teaspoon salt

Instructions

1. Preheat the oven to 375 F.
2. Place chocolate chips, ¼ cup coconut oil in a bowl placed over boiling water. Stir well while melting the chocolate.
3. In a separate bowl whisk sugar and flax eggs with an electric mixer.
4. Gradually add in ¾ cup coconut oil, beets, cooled chocolate mixture and vanilla. Transfer to a large bowl.
5. To the large bowl add sifted flour, baking soda, salt and combine well, transfer to a greased floured 10-cup Bundt pan.
6. Bake for 60 minutes. Remove from the oven and let it cool.
7. Dust with powdered sugar, drizzle chocolate syrup and top with fresh whipped cream.
8. Once done, serve.

Nutritional information (per serving): 391 calories; 24 g fat; 42 g total carbs; 3 g protein

Vegan Pie with Cranberry and Apple Filling

Cooking Time: 1 hour 15 minutes

Servings: 8

Ingredients

Cranberry sauce
- 2 cups cranberries
- ½ cup water
- 1/3 cup maple syrup
- zest 1 orange + juice

Apple Filling
- 4 cups sliced & peeled apples
- 1/3 cup sugar
- ½ teaspoon cinnamon
- ¼ teaspoon pumpkin pie spice
- 1 ½ tablespoons all-purpose flour
- ¼ teaspoon salt

Crust
- 2 cups all-purpose flour
- 2/3 + 2 tablespoons cold vegan butter
- ¼ teaspoon cinnamon
- ¼ teaspoon pumpkin pie spice
- 6 tablespoons ice water
- 1 teaspoon salt

Instructions

1. Preheat the oven 400 F.
2. To a skillet placed over medium heat add cranberries water and maple syrup. Bring the mixture to a boil. Reduce heat, let it cook for 10 minutes while stirring until it thickens.
3. Remove from heat, add in orange zest and juice. Set aside.
4. To prepare the apple filling, to a baking dish add apples, cinnamon, salt, sugar, pumpkin pie spice and flour.
5. To make the crust, in a large bowl combine flour, salt, pumpkin pie spice and cinnamon.
6. Add vegan butter and combine well.
7. Gradually add ice water until a dough is formed, mold the dough and divide into 2 balls, one larger than the other.
8. Take the larger ball and roll into a large crust, drape it over a pie pan, trim the excess dough hanging off the edges.
9. Add cranberry sauce with the apple filling to the crust. Set aside.
10. Roll out the remaining dough, cut into strips and form a lattice top, place on the pie and press down the edges, sprinkle sugar and cinnamon on top.
11. Place pie in the oven and bake for 45 minutes. Set aside to cook for 5 hours.
12.   Once done, serve.

Nutritional information (per serving): 230 calories; 1,6 g fat; 52 g total carbs; 4 g protein

Chocolate Pudding with Avocados

Cooking Time: 10 minutes　　　　　　**Servings:** 4

Ingredients

- 1 ½ ripe avocados
- 1 ripe banana
- ½ cup cacao powder
- ¼ cup agave
- ¼ cup unsweetened almond milk
- ¼ cup almond butter crunchy, optional topping

Instructions

1. To a food processor add avocados, bananas, cocoa powder, agave and almond milk. Pulse until smooth.
2. Serve and divide the pudding between serving glasses.
3. Top with favorite toppings like almond butter and mix it in.
4. Once done, serve.

Nutritional information (per serving): 295 calories; 29 g fat; 26 g total carbs; 7 g protein

Meal Plan

WEEK 1, 3 Shopping List

Vegetables and Fruits
- [ ] 4 potatoes
- [ ] 8 onions
- [ ] 1 red onion
- [ ] 1 sweet onion
- [ ] 12 bell peppers
- [ ] 1 bunch kale
- [ ] 13 garlic cloves
- [ ] 1 packet mixed greens
- [ ] 1 handful parsley
- [ ] 1 handful cilantro
- [ ] 1 avocado
- [ ] 2 cups blueberries or mixed berries
- [ ] Fresh ginger
- [ ] 1 lemon
- [ ] 1 ripe banana
- [ ] 5 ¼ cups carrots
- [ ] 1 cup green cabbage
- [ ] 3 scallions
- [ ] 1 cup red cabbage
- [ ] 3/4 cup edamame soy beans
- [ ] 1 avocado, chopped
- [ ] 1 Roma tomato, chopped
- [ ] 1 handful arugula
- [ ] 1 jalapeño
- [ ] 1 cup flat leaf parsley
- [ ] 1 handful fresh basil leaves
- [ ] 1 tomato
- [ ] 1 bunch broccoli rabe
- [ ] 1 cup mushrooms
- [ ] 1 lime
- [ ] 2 handfuls arugula

Soy Products
- [ ] 16 oz tempeh
- [ ] 24 oz package tofu

Pasta, Bread, Nuts, and Grains
- [ ] 8 oz. package tempeh, diced
- [ ] 3 slices gluten-free bread
- [ ] ¾ cup whole almonds
- [ ] 2 cups gluten free rolled oats
- [ ] ½ cup dried blueberries

- [ ] ½ cup pistachios
- [ ] ⅓ cup walnuts
- [ ] ⅓ cup pepitas
- [ ] 5 tablespoons chia seeds
- [ ] 1 cup dry golden quinoa
- [ ] ½ cup dry millet
- [ ] 2 cups hazelnuts, roughly chopped and toasted
- [ ] 1 cup steel-cut oats
- [ ] ¾ cup rolled oats
- [ ] 3 tablespoons dried cranberries
- [ ] 3 ½ cups cashews
- [ ] 1 cup brown lentils
- [ ] 3 slices bread, whole wheat
- [ ] 1 tablespoon raw walnuts
- [ ] 4 hamburger buns
- [ ] 1 ½ cups green French lentils
- [ ] ½ cup breadcrumbs
- [ ] 1 cup quinoa
- [ ] 1/2 cup white quinoa, uncooked
- [ ] 3/4 cup pecans
- [ ] 8 medjool dates
- [ ] 6 taco shells

Canned and Frozen
- [ ] 4 tablespoons capers
- [ ] 2 cans chickpeas
- [ ] 15 oz. canned green or red kidney beans
- [ ] 15 oz. canned lentils
- [ ] 2 (15.5 oz.) cans chickpeas
- [ ] 5-6 sun-dried tomatoes in oil
- [ ] 1 (14 oz.) can tomato sauce
- [ ] 1 (28 oz.) can kidney beans
- [ ] 1 (28 oz.) can tomatoes
- [ ] 1 ½ cups corn kernels
- [ ] 2 (15 oz.) cans black beans
- [ ] 3 (14 oz.) cans white beans

Sauces and Liquids
- [ ] Olive oil
- [ ] 6 oz. soy milk
- [ ] 1 cup almond milk

- [ ] Vanilla extract
- [ ] White vinegar
- [ ] ½ cup pumpkin puree
- [ ] Flax eggs
- [ ] Coconut oil
- [ ] Pure maple syrup
- [ ] ¼ cup unsweetened apple sauce
- [ ] 1 cup almond butter
- [ ] 1 cup vegan yogurt
- [ ] 1 cup unsweetened vanilla almond milk
- [ ] Agave
- [ ] Tahini
- [ ] 1 tablespoon caper brine
- [ ] Balsamic vinegar
- [ ] Peanut butter
- [ ] Hot sauce
- [ ] Tamari
- [ ] 1 tablespoon Dijon mustard
- [ ] 1/4 cup apple cider vinegar
- [ ] Sriracha
- [ ] 1 teaspoon sugar
- [ ] Grapeseed oil
- [ ] 1/4 teaspoon dried rosemary
- [ ] 1/4 teaspoon dried oregano
- [ ] 1/4 teaspoon dried basil

- [ ] 1 cup vanilla coconut yogurt
- [ ] 1 tablespoon psyllium husk
- [ ] ½ teaspoon raw ground vanilla bean

Spices and Powders
- [ ] Paprika
- [ ] Nutritional yeast
- [ ] Salt
- [ ] Pepper
- [ ] 1 scoop vanilla protein
- [ ] 2 tablespoons flax meal
- [ ] 1 cup white whole wheat flour
- [ ] Cinnamon
- [ ] Baking powder
- [ ] Baking soda
- [ ] Pumpkin pie spice
- [ ] ⅓ cup ground flaxseed
- [ ] ¼ cup sunflower seeds
- [ ] ¼ teaspoon nutmeg
- [ ] 2 tablespoons PB Fit powder
- [ ] Turmeric
- [ ] 2 tablespoons coconut sugar
- [ ] 2 tablespoons cashew butter

Day 1

Breakfast
Skillet Potato and Tempeh Hash
Lunch
High Protein Salad
Dinner
Tomato-Braised Lentils
Snack/Dessert
Quinoa Brittle

Day 2

Breakfast
High Protein Vegan French Toast
Lunch
Tempeh Tacos
Dinner
Tomato-Braised Lentils
Snack/Dessert
Quinoa Brittle

Day 3

Breakfast
Pumpkin Chia Pancakes
Lunch
Chickpeas Edamame Salad
Dinner
Caesar White Bean Burgers
Snack/Dessert
Protein Black Bean Lime Dip

Day 4

Breakfast
Blueberry Bliss Breakfast Bars Raw
Lunch
Avocado White Bean Salad
Dinner
Caesar White Bean Burgers
Snack/Dessert
Protein Black Bean Lime Dip

Day 5

Breakfast
Chickpea Scramble Breakfast Bowl
Lunch
Arugula Lentil Salad
Dinner
Steamed Trout with Red Bean and Chilli Salsa
Snack/Dessert
Classic Baked Cheesecake

Day 6

Breakfast
Grain Salad with Blueberries Hazelnuts Lemon
Lunch
Maple Tempeh with Carrot Slaw
Dinner
Quinoa Stuffed Peppers
Snack/Dessert
Classic Baked Cheesecake

Day 7

Breakfast
Peanut Butter Chia Overnight Oats
Lunch
Tofu Chili
Dinner
Tofu Chickpea Stir-Fry
Snack/Dessert
Classic Baked Cheesecak

Vegetables and Fruits

- [ ] Parsley
- [ ] 26 garlic cloves
- [ ] 5 whole baby potatoes
- [ ] 1 bunch kale
- [ ] 2 bell peppers
- [ ] 2 avocados
- [ ] Cilantro
- [ ] 3 bananas
- [ ] 3 shallots
- [ ] 2 tomatoes
- [ ] 1 poblano pepper
- [ ] 6 onions
- [ ] 3 Roma tomatoes
- [ ] 9 carrots
- [ ] 1 onion, diced
- [ ] 3 sweet potatoes
- [ ] 1 bell pepper
- [ ] 1 small white onion, diced
- [ ] 1 cup zucchini
- [ ] 1 1/2 cups asparagus
- [ ] 1 cup packed kale or spinach
- [ ] 3 cups pumpkin
- [ ] 1 red chili pepper
- [ ] 1 small zucchini
- [ ] 3 lbs. pumpkin
- [ ] Ginger
- [ ] 1 chili, chopped
- [ ] 1/2 white onion
- [ ] 1/2 white onion
- [ ] 1 brown onion
- [ ] 1 scallion
- [ ] 1 small Serrano or jalapeño pepper
- [ ] 1 lemon
- [ ] 7 cups blueberries

Soy Products

- [ ] 32-oz extra-firm tofu
- [ ] 20 oz. tempeh
- [ ] 1 packet gluten-free tempeh

Pasta, Bread, Nuts, and Grains

- [ ] 4 flour gluten-free tortillas
- [ ] 2 slices sprouted wheat bread
- [ ] 1 tablespoon hemp seeds
- [ ] 1 tablespoon unsalted sunflower seeds
- [ ] 6 slices gluten free crusty bread
- [ ] ½ cup quinoa
- [ ] 10 small corn tortillas
- [ ] 5 tablespoons chia seeds
- [ ] 1 cup old-fashioned rolled oats
- [ ] 1 cup brown lentils
- [ ] 1/4 cup white quinoa
- [ ] ½ cup quick cook faro
- [ ] ½ cup red lentils
- [ ] 1/3 cup lentils or split peas
- [ ] 2 cups brown rice
- [ ] 1 cup red lentils
- [ ] ⅓ cup mixed raw seeds
- [ ] ½ cup unsweetened coconut
- [ ] 3 tablespoons hemp seeds
- [ ] 1 cup (about 13) Medjool dates
- [ ] 2 cups raw pecan halves
- [ ] 2 cups oats
- [ ] 1 cup almonds
- [ ] 2 tablespoons flax seed
- [ ] 8 medjool dates, pitted and soaked in warm water for ½ an hour
- [ ] 2 cups chickpeas
- [ ] 1/2 cup quinoa

Canned and Frozen

- [ ] ½ cup jarred roasted bell pepper
- [ ] 1 tablespoon pitted Kalamata olives
- [ ] 6 (15 oz.) cans black beans
- [ ] 1 (15 oz.) can diced tomatoes or tomato sauce
- [ ] 1/2 cup salsa
- [ ] 1 (28 oz.) can tomatoes, diced
- [ ] 1/2 cup peas, frozen
- [ ] 2 (15 oz.) cans tomato sauce
- [ ] 1 whole chipotle in adobo sauce, canned plus 1 tablespoon sauce
- [ ] 1 (28-oz.) can crushed tomatoes
- [ ] 8 oz. full fat coconut cream
- [ ] 2 cups frozen berries

Sauces and Liquids

- [ ] Oil
- [ ] Hummus
- [ ] 3 cups almond milk
- [ ] Peanut butter
- [ ] Maple syrup
- [ ] Vanilla extract
- [ ] 1 batch of berry chia jam
- [ ] Vegetable oil
- [ ] 16 cups vegetable broth + 1 1/2 cups

- 3 tablespoons white miso paste
- 1 tablespoon ketchup
- 1/3 cup rice vinegar
- 1 teaspoon tamari
- 4 tablespoons sake
- 3 tablespoons soy sauce
- 1/2 cup coconut milk
- 1 tablespoon tomato paste

Spices and Powders

- Chili powder
- Cumin
- Nutritional yeast
- Sea salt
- Chili powder
- 2 tablespoons cacao powder
- 2 scoops vital proteins collagen
- 2 teaspoons maca powder
- Smoked paprika
- Sweet paprika
- Cinnamon
- 1 teaspoon sugar
- 1 chai tea bag
- ½ tablespoon coconut palm sugar
- 1 teaspoon vanilla extract

- Smoked paprika
- 1 scoop vanilla protein powder
- Bay leaves
- Pepper
- Dried thyme
- Garlic powder
- Italian seasoning
- Red pepper flakes
- Dried oregano
- Turmeric
- 1 cinnamon stick
- Sunflower oil
- Sesame oil
- 2 teaspoons cornstarch dissolved in 4 teaspoons of water
- 1 1/2 tablespoons garam masala
- ¼ cup hemp protein powder
- ½ teaspoon vanilla
- 2 tablespoons cacao powder
- Cinnamon
- ¼ cup cacao

Day 1

Breakfast
Scrambled Tofu Breakfast Burrito
Lunch
Black Bean and Sweet Potato Chili
Dinner
Tomato-Braised Lentils
Snack/Dessert
Hemp Protein Date Bars

Day 2

Breakfast
Hummus Toast
Lunch
Black Bean and Sweet Potato Chili
Dinner
Smoky Tempeh Burrito Bowls
Snack/Dessert
Hemp Protein Date Bars

Day 3

Breakfast
Chocolate Peanut Butter Smoothie Bowl
Lunch
Black Bean Soup
Dinner
Sweet and Sour Tempeh
Snack/Dessert
Blueberry Crisp

Day 4

Breakfast
Greek Chickpeas On Toast
Lunch
Vegetable Quinoa Minestrone
Dinner
Sweet and Sour Tempeh
Snack/Dessert
Blueberry Crisp

Day 5

Breakfast
Quinoa With Chai Spiced Almond Milk Cinnamon
Lunch
Quinoa Black Bean Pumpkin Soup
Dinner
Korean Braised Tofu
Snack/Dessert
Maple Candied Pecans

Day 6

Breakfast
Spicy Scrambled Tofu Breakfast Tacos
Lunch
Turmeric Lentil Soup
Dinner
Korean Braised Tofu
Snack/Dessert
Maple Candied Pecans

Day 7

Breakfast
Peanut Butter Jelly Overnight Oats
Lunch
Miso, Lentil, and Pumpkin Soup
Dinner
Red Lentil Tikka Masala
Snack/Dessert
Plant Based Peanut Butter Cream Sweet
 Potato Brow

Printed in Great Britain
by Amazon